NATIVE AMERICAN LEGENDS OF THE GREAT LAKES AND THE MISSISSIPPI VALLEY

NATIVE AMERICAN LEGENDS OF THE GREAT LAKES AND THE MISSISSIPPI VALLEY

Selected and Edited by Katharine B. Judson

Introduced by Peter Iverson

NORTHERN ILLINOIS UNIVERSITY PRESS DEKALB 2000

Published by the Northern Illinois University Press, DeKalb, Illinois 60115

Manufactured in the United States using acid-free paper

Paperback cover and text design by Julia Fauci

Library of Congress Cataloging-in-Publication Data

Judson, Katharine Berry.

[Myths and legends of the Mississippi Valley and the Great Lakes]

Native American legends of the Great Lakes and the Mississippi Valley / selected and edited by Katharine B. Judson ; introduced by Peter Iverson.

p. c.m.

Originally published: Myths and legends of the Mississippi Valley and the Great Lakes. Chicago : A.C. McClurg, 1914.

Includes bibliographical references and index.

ISBN 0-87580-250-8 (clothbound : alk. paper) — ISBN 0-87580-581-7 (pbk. : alk. paper)

1. Indians of North America—Great Lakes Region—-Folklore. 2. Indians of North America—Mississippi River Valley—Folklore. 3. Legends—Great Lakes Region. 4. Legends—Mississippi River Valley. I. Title.

E78.G7J83 2000

398.2'089'97077—dc21 99-052766

CONTENTS

PART III: RABBIT, LYNX, OWL

PART V: SUN, MOON, STARS

PREFACE

Katharine B. Judson

Mystery, magic, and manitoes abound in the land of Hiawatha, in the land of Ojibwas, among the green islands, graceful and beautiful, lying amidst the dancing blue waters when the sun shines over Gitche Gomee, the Great Water.[1] Manitoes, great and mighty, lived in the cool depths on the mighty forests, in the rivers and lakes, and even in the snows of winter. And adventures there were in those early days amongst these islands of the North, when manitoes directed the affairs of men.

But the animal fathers lived upon the earth before there came the "two-legged walkers." There were many animals. There were many beavers. It was the beavers who made Gitche Gomee, the Great Water. They made it by building two dams. The first they built at the Grand Sault, and the second was five leagues below. When Great Hare came up the river, he said, "This must not be so." Therefore he stepped upon the first dam. But he was in haste. He did not break it down; therefore there are now great falls and whirlpools at that place. But at the second dam, Great Hare stepped upon it mightily; therefore there are now few falls and only a little swirling water at that place. Great Hare was very mighty. When he chased Beaver he stepped across a bay eight leagues wide.

Around Michilimackinack was the land of Great Hare. There, amongst the green islets, under the cool shade of wide spreading trees, where fish leaped above the rippling waters, he made the first fish net. He made it after watching Spider weave a web for catching flies.

It was Wenibojo,[2] who, in Ojibwa land, discovered the wild rice and taught the Indians to use it. He first pointed out the low grassy islands in the lakes, waving their bright green leaves and spikes of yellowish-green blossoms. He showed them how to cut paths through the wild-rice beds before the grain was ripe, and later, to beat it into their canoes. He told them always to gather the wild rice before a storm, else the wind would blow it all into the water. Therefore the Indians use wild rice in all their feasts. They even taught the white men to use it.

When the snows of winter lay deep upon the forests of the North, when ice covered lakes and rivers, then the story tellers of the Ojibwas, as of all other Indian tribes, told the tales of the olden times, when manitoes lived upon the earth, and when the animal fathers roamed through the forest. But such stories are not told in summer. All the woods and shores, all the bays and islands, are, in summer, the home of keen-hearing spirits, who like not to have Indians talking about them. But when the deep snows come, then the spirits are more drowsy. Then the Indians, when North West rattles the flaps of the wigwams, and wild animals hide in the shelter of the deep forest, tell their tales. All winter they tell them, while the fires burn in the wigwams—tell them until the frogs croak in the spring.

Tales they tell of how Gitche Manito, the Good One, taught the Indians how to plant the Indian corn, how to strip and bury Mondamin, and how to gather the corn in the month of falling leaves, that there may be food in the camps when the snows of winter come. Tales they tell of Gitche Manedo, the Evil One, who brings only distress and sickness—tales of the land of Hiawatha. Mystery and magic lay all about them.

It is a far cry from the stories of the North along the banks of the Mississippi, from that land of long winters, through the country of the mound builders, to the sunnier Southland; yet from north to south, around the glimmering Indian fires, grouped eager men and women and children, listening to the story tellers.

But quite different are the tales of the Southland—of the Cherokees, Biloxis, and Chitimachas. They are stories of wild turkeys, of persimmons and raccoons, and of the spirits which dwell in the mountain places where none dare go. Stories also are they of Brer Rabbit and the tar wolf, which came from Indian slaves working in the fields in early days, through the Negro slaves working beside them, to the children of the white men.

▲▲▲

It is a loss to American literature that so much of the legendary history of these Indian tribes has gone, beyond hope of recovery. Exquisite in color, poetical in feeling, these legends of sun, moon, and stars, of snow, ice, lightning, thunders, the winds, the life of the forest birds and animals about them, and the longing to understand the why and the how of life—all which we have only in fragments. Longfellow's work shows the wonderful beauty of these northern legends, nor has he done violence to any of them in making them poetical. His picture of the departure of Hiawatha, the lone figure standing stately and solemn, as the canoe drifted out towards the glowing sunset, while from the shore, in the shadow of the forest, came the low Indian chant, mingling with the sighing of the pine trees, is truly Indian. For the mystical and poetical is strong in the Indian nature.

As in all the other volumes of this series, no effort has been made to ornament or amplify these legends in the effort to make them "literary," or give them "literary charm." They must speak for themselves. What editing has been done has been in simplifying them, and freeing them from the verbose setting in which many were found. For in this section of the country, settled before it was realized that there was an Indian literature, the original work of noting down the myths was very imperfectly done.

Thanks are due to the work of Albert E. Jenks, on the wild-rice Indians of the upper lakes; to James Mooney, for the myths of the Cherokees; to George Catlin, for some of the upper Mississippi legends; to the well-known but almost inaccessible work of Schoolcraft, and to others.

Notes

1. Gitche Gomee is Lake Superior.

2. Wenibojo is only a variation of the name also give as Manabush. Both are identical with Hiawatha.

INTRODUCTION

Peter Iverson

This book is more than it initially appears to be. It was first published in 1914 under the title *Myths and Legends of the Mississippi Valley and the Great Lakes* as part of a series of books that Katharine Berry Judson compiled for A. C. McClurg Publishing Company. No doubt the original titles were chosen to emphasize the regional appeal of each volume. Yet this book is not an anthology of folk stories loosely organized by region but a collection of American Indian stories. Thus at that time in our history when American Indians commonly were portrayed and perceived as vanishing peoples, they also vanished from the titles of books devoted to their culture. That omission has been corrected in this edition. Then there is the matter of the first three words of the original title. To many readers, "myths and legends" will suggest a collection of stories that are both false and irrelevant. Today *myth* often refers to something that is not true, while *legend* suggests something that is not only not true but is either too good to be true or so fantastic in nature that it only represents a kind of frivolous diversion. My dictionary links *legend* and *myth* as synonyms, noting that they generally involve "gods, heroes, imaginary animals, etc. current since primitive times, the purpose of which is to attempt to explain some belief or natural phenomenon." Judson blended these terms, for she knew these stories were not simply "tales" but that they formed an Indian literature that was important on its own terms as well as in relation to American literature.

The bias toward written rather than oral sources remains

entrenched in American thought, but, as Native individuals have always told the rest of us, oral sources are critical if we are going to begin to try to understand the richness and the complexity of Indian cultures. The best work in the field of American Indian history incorporates oral history and oral tradition. Students of the stories are starting to reveal to us just how much we can learn from these accounts, helping us to understand that we cannot separate Indian lives from Indian stories.[1] Through the centuries stories provided the means through which American Indian children learned about their world. Through stories told by older relatives, they began their participation in a school in which they would always be enrolled. A child began to learn about who he or she was and to whom he or she belonged, began to learn about proper behavior, began to learn about the right way in which to live.

Not too long ago Native children were born into a community in which they would remain throughout their lives. Parents, other relatives, indeed all members of the group had a vested interest in the education and upbringing of a child. Before the advent of written languages, before the world made possible by the invention of the printing press, one turned to the elders to learn about how the world came to be and how one should behave in it. All over North America, the older people fashioned stories to entertain and to teach the young. There were no short cuts to becoming wise; there were no alternatives to listening. You could not rely upon a CD-ROM or depend upon a video for instruction. The stories constituted your library, your archive, your heritage.

Katharine Berry Judson understood this significance of myths, legends, and stories. She graduated from Cornell

University in 1904, at a time when few women had the opportunity to obtain post-secondary education. Even though she held a degree from a prestigious educational institution, Judson nonetheless confronted a society that limited the options for talented and trained women. Taking one of the few avenues available to her, she decided to become a librarian. Like countless men and women in the nineteenth and twentieth centuries, Judson concluded that she might have more opportunities if she moved to the western part of the United States. She worked for two years as a librarian in Kalispell, Montana, then relocated to Seattle, where she accepted a position as chief of the periodical department for the public library. Aided by the Loretta Denny Fellowship, she enrolled in the M.A. program in history at the University of Washington. She sprinted through the requirements for the degree, completing in one year her course work and her thesis on "Fur Trading Forts of Old Oregon, 1810–1834." Later she worked as a research assistant in the history department at Washington and contributed articles to the *American Historical Review, Century Magazine,* and the *Oregon Historical Quarterly*. She wanted to share with others her fascination with the heritage of America.

Judson differed from most Americans of this era in her appreciation of America's multicultural heritage. She realized that this heritage had been informed and enriched by the stories and teachings of many different peoples, including the first inhabitants of the land we now call the United States. Because she had graduate training in history and because she worked in a university library, she knew about and appreciated the efforts by various individuals in the late nineteenth and early twentieth centuries to record, transcribe, edit, and interpret traditional American Indian stories. At the same time, she saw much of this pioneering ethnological study going to waste. Few people had heard of the Bureau of American Ethnology, and fewer still would bother to read its reports. The work of Henry Schoolcraft and James Mooney would be valued by later students of American Indian societies, but much of what they uncovered remained ignored in their own time. Katharine Berry Judson decided to do something about this situation. This book is an integral part her efforts to make Native American stories available to a much wider audience.

Yet, like most Americans then, Judson viewed Indian cultures as frozen in time and doomed inevitably to continuing erosion and eventual disappearance. The original edition of this book was published in the year a man named Ishi died. Labeled "California's last wild Indian," Ishi became a celebrity in his final years. Literally the last of his tribe, hungry, and alone, he had come into the small town of Oroville, California, seeking food and shelter. The town authorities jailed him. Ishi was rescued from captivity by anthropologist Albert Kroeber of the University of California, who soon provided him with a name ("Ishi" means "man" in the Yahi language) and a new home. In return, Ishi gave the Berkeley anthropologist a detailed knowledge of Yahi language and culture. Ishi's home became the confines of the California Museum of Anthropology rather than those of the Oroville jail, and, with the exception of one return trip, he remained removed from the country of his people. Ishi's passing in 1911 sounded the same note as the photographs of Edward Curtis, who carried out a protracted campaign to capture images of what he believed to be disappearing cultures. Curtis's most famous image was entitled "The Vanishing Race." "The thought which this picture is meant to convey," he wrote, "is that the Indians as a race, already shorn of their tribal strength and stripped of their primitive dress, are passing into the darkness of an unknown future."

Judson collected these stories, then, during the same generation that Curtis took his photographs and sculptor James Fraser created his popular image of "The End of the Trail"—the defeated Indian warrior slumped over on horseback. In the context of this era it is not surprising that she chose to conclude the anthology with a Wyandot story of "The Coming of the White Man." After the people had given them "skin clothes," this story relates, "The White men went away. They came back many times. They asked the Indians for room to put a chair on the land. So it was given. But soon they began to pull the lacing out of the bottom and to walk inland with it. They have not yet come to the end of the string."

"It is a loss to American literature," Judson asserts in her preface, "that so much of the legendary history of these Indian tribes has gone, beyond hope of recovery." In part because of her work, her fears turned out to be as unfounded as the more general perspective that held the Indians to be "a vanishing race," but we can appreciate her assumptions, for they indeed constituted the conventional wisdom of the time. This anthology was the fourth of Judson's volumes to appear in print, preceded by books devoted to the myths and legends of Alaska and the Pacific Northwest, of California and the Old Southwest, and of North America more generally. In each of these books Judson readily acknowledged that she built upon the foundation established by others, and it is not too difficult to trace her sources. Once she had found an appropriate story, Judson generally modified it through condensing the narrative, but she often borrowed passages word for word or only slightly paraphrased what she had found in a Bureau of American Ethnology report or some comparable source.

The Menominee story about the Catfish and the Moose, included in this book, furnishes an instructive case in point. Compare the version provided by Walter James Hoffman in *The Menomini Indians,* a Bureau of American Ethnology volume published in 1896, with Judson's rendition.

Hoffman: "Once when the Catfish were assembled in the water an old chief said to them, 'I have often seen a Moose come to the edge of the water to eat grass; let us watch for him, and kill and eat him. He always comes when the sun is a little way up in the sky.'

"The Catfish who heard this agreed to go and attack the Moose; so they went to watch. They were scattered everywhere among the grass and rushes, when the Moose came slowly along picking grass. He waded down into the water, where he began to feast. The catfish all watched to see what the old chief would do, and presently one of them worked his way slowly through the grass to where the Moose's leg was, when he thrust his spear into it. Then the Moose said, 'What is it that has thrown a spear into my leg?' and looking down he saw the Catfish, when he immediately began to trample upon them with his hoofs, killing a good number of them, while those that escaped swam down the river as fast as they could. The Catfish still carry spears, but their heads have never recovered from the flattening they received when they were tramped by the Moose into the mud."

Judson: "Once when the Catfish were all together in one place in the water, the Catfish chief said, 'I have often seen a moose come to the edge of the water to eat grass. Let us watch for him and kill him and eat him. He always comes when the sun is a little way up in the sky.'

"The Catfish agreed to attack Moose. So they went to watch. They crept everywhere in among the grass and rushes when Moose came down to the water's edge, slowly picking at the grass. All the tribe watched to see what the Catfish chief would do. He slipped slowly through the marshy grass to where Moose was standing. He thrust his spear into Moose's leg.

"Moose said, 'Who has thrust a spear into my leg?' He looked down and saw the Catfish tribe. At once he began to trample upon them with his hoofs. He killed many, but others escaped and swam down the river.

"Catfish still carry spears, but their heads are flat, because Moose trampled them down in the mud."

This example gives a good sense of Judson's approach. We can see that she could take passages directly from the original account but that she also could alter and shorten the text. Judson offers a rendition that is slightly abbreviated and somewhat more direct. The beginning of the Menominee story about the origin of tobacco offers another illustration. First, here is how Hoffman rendered it: "One day Ma'nabush was passing by a high mountain, when he detected a delightful odor which seemed to come from a crevice in the cliffs. On going closer he found the mountain inhabited by a giant who was known to be the keeper of tobacco. Ma'nabush then went to the mouth of a cavern, which he entered, and following the passage which led down into the very center of the mountain he found a large chamber occupied by a giant, who asked him in a very stern manner what he wanted."

Now, consider Judson's rendition: "One day when Manabush

was passing by a high mountain, a fragrant odor came to him from a crevice in the cliffs. He went closer. Then he knew that in the mountain was a giant who was the Keeper of Tobacco. He entered the mouth of a cave, going through a long tunnel to the center of the mountain. There in a great wigwam was the giant. The giant said sternly, 'What do you want?'" Judson's more direct, straightforward style reads more clearly and cleanly than the often stilted transcriptions or compositions that formed the basis for her work.

The language is one element that encourages a continued readership for these stories, but the tales have other appealing qualities as well. As did other peoples all over the world, American Indians employed stories to explain the creation of the world and the origins of their communities, to delineate the presence of particular animals or the importance of certain crops, and to offer often whimsical explanations for a particular bird's or animal's appearance. These universal qualities appeal to readers and listeners almost regardless of background or upbringing. One can read them or hear them and appreciate the kind of imagination and creativity that gave them being.

Rereading this book encouraged me to consider again how people all over the world grow up with and grow through stories. I also began to learn about the world through stories. My mother grew up in eastern Kansas and in central Michigan. She passed along to me and my brothers her well-worn Bedtime Story Books by the naturalist Thornton W. Burgess, and no doubt our children will likewise acquaint their children with Old Mother West Wind, Jimmy Skunk, Chatterer the Red Squirrel, and Ol' Mistah Buzzard. These books underscored that actions had consequences and that, if you were smart but arrogant, like Granny

Fox, then Old Man Coyote just might teach you a lesson.

My father's fascination with words eventually led him to teach children's literature at Stanford. He and his irrepressible coauthor Sam Sebesta once wrote that literature "spreads warmth in much the same way as does music, painting, or sculpture. Like music, literature brings the stimulation of sound and rhythm. Like painting, it brings the illumination of imagery and design. Like sculpture, literature brings the awareness of texture and space. When it is well conveyed, literature like all art, leaves a lasting radiance." Literature, they say, has a number of purposes: "providing entertainment, developing insight through information, presenting human options, encouraging empathy, and heightening awareness of beauty." The stories included in this volume surely fulfill this definition.[2]

In Judson's time, however, American Indian stories were rarely considered literature, which in part explains why the long shadow of Henry Wadsworth Longfellow falls upon Judson's preface. Today few children are compelled to participate in school pageants reciting *The Song of Hiawatha,* yet in the nineteenth century Longfellow's purple poetry set one standard for Indian stories. In 1855 Longfellow completed his epic poem, which he modeled upon the Finnish *Kalevala.* He employed the work of Henry Rowe Schoolcraft, the tireless student and collector of Indian stories, who had gathered many stories about the Ojibwa (also Anishinabe or Chippewa) culture hero Manabozho (who appears here as Manabush). Instead of calling his subject Manabozho, Longfellow decided to call him another four syllable name: Hiawatha.[3] This name sounded better to the New England poet, but in fact Hiawatha is an Iroquois figure with no connection to the Ojibwe. Although Longfellow's poetry was enormously popular, even in the nineteenth century it became the subject of parody and abuse, and Judson felt compelled to defend the poet. "Longfellow's work," she asserts, "shows the wonderful beauty of these northern legends, nor has he done violence to any of them in making them poetical. . . . For the mystical and poetical is strong in the Indian nature." Today the term "the Indian nature" gives us pause, but in fairness to Judson we must acknowledge that most Americans in the early twentieth century (and more than a few Americans at the end of the twentieth century) tended to overgeneralize about "the Indian." They lumped Indians together regardless of place or circumstance and paid no attention to distinctive dimensions of individual communities. Despite Judson's defense of Longfellow, when editing these stories she had the good sense, as she put it, not "to make them 'literary,' or give them 'literary charm.' They must speak for themselves." On that fundamental point she was absolutely correct.

Longfellow and others simplified and romanticized and misconstrued such stories. It is important for us to understand that these stories are more than simple tales and that they had and have cultural significance for the Native American communities who told them. One of their most compelling features is the manner in which they speak to the complicated interrelationships between humans and other living things. Children learned from these stories that humans were not superior to animals and birds and that human origin was related to the beginnings of these other beings. They were taught that the survival of the people depended upon their proper treatment of these other creatures. "Now in those days," goes the Chitimacha story, "the animals took part in the councils of men. They gave advice to men, being wiser. Each animal took especial care of the Chitimachas. Therefore the Indians respect the animals which gave good advice to their ancestors, and this aids them even today in time of need." This perspective is clearly quite different from the Euro-American teachings that placed people separate from and superior to birds and animals and that helped encourage the disappearance of various species and the near extermination of others. Although Indians hunted animals, most believed that the animals gave themselves up rather than being outsmarted or overpowered. They would acknowledge the gift of the meat and the hide and express proper ritual appreciation. The contrast between the Native and Euro-American perspective on hunting the buffalo yields a vivid reminder about differences in cultural upbringing as well as in the workings of economies.

The stories collected here also emphasize the importance of place. When one thinks about the tremendous disruptions to Indian life in the region encompassed by the stories included in this volume, one appreciates the poignancy of these accounts for Native listeners. During the time these tales were being collected, Indian communities faced an onslaught on their lives and lands. Our history books still pay far more attention to the battles on the plains and in the Southwest that erupted in the latter part of the nineteenth century than to other kinds of battles waged over a longer period of time by Indian groups in the Midwest and in the South. As did the more publicized confrontations, these struggles involved the land itself—the ability of the peoples to remain in territories that they believed they must inhabit. The prospect of removal from particular regions raised the specter of cultural annihilation. The late nineteenth and early twentieth centuries witnessed a devastating assault upon the Indian estate. Native American communities faced demands by both individual Euro-American "settlers" and companies determined to wrest control over the natural resources situated on these lands. These people and these interests cared little about the Menominee account of the origin of maple sugar; they wanted the trees for their own purposes, regardless of the social, cultural, and economic importance of the trees for Indians.

The map of the Great Lakes and Mississippi valley today reveals that despite all the attempts to eradicate Indian land holdings, the continuing existence of Indian communities cannot be denied. At the same time, because of land allotment and other ill-advised federal policies, American Indian acreage became fragmented and reduced. Indian peoples still struggle for recognition of their rights to use the lands and waters of their home country in the ways they deem appropriate. An 1837 treaty, for example, gave the Mille Lacs Band of Chippewa from Minnesota the right to hunt and fish on public land. This right remained contested through the decades. The state of Minnesota argued that its statehood in 1858 took away from the tribe the right to hunt and fish without any kind of state restriction. In March 1999, by the narrowest of margins, the United States Supreme Court sided with the Ojibwe people. Thomas Maulson, chairman of the Lac du Flambeau Band of Chippewa in Wisconsin, has fought similar battles in his state. He said the Supreme Court decision marked "a good day again in Indian country" and observed that "we are starting to acknowledge the fact that history is important and that treaty rights are reserved for Native people." This victory, then, testified to the possibility of triumph. Yet the narrow 5–4 vote in the court mirrored existing divisions about the nature of Native

American rights and demonstrates the necessity for continued efforts to forge a secure future.

So the stories and the people continue, but the battles are never over. More Americans now realize that our national heritage is truly multicultural, but there are forces that insist upon a narrow and incomplete interpretation of that heritage. The American Indian presence upon the land at the end of the twentieth century is cause for celebration, even as the patterns of history remind us that each era presents new challenges. Entering a new century, Native American elders tell the next generations that history's lessons must be remembered. They say that the treaties must always be defended. They emphasize that the stories must continue to be told.

Notes

1. It is altogether appropriate that Julie Cruikshank entitled her pathbreaking collection of the stories told by three Yukon elder women *Life Lived Like a Story: Life Stories of Three Yukon Native Elders* (Lincoln: University of Nebraska Press, 1990).

2. Sam Leaton Sebesta and William J. Iverson, Introduction to *Literature For Thursday's Child* (Chicago: Science Research Associates, 1975), 2, 19.

3. See the introduction by Daniel Aaron to Henry Wadsworth Longfellow, *The Song of Hiawatha* (1855; rpt., London: J. M. Dent & Sons, 1992).

4. Associated Press wire story, March 25, 1999; *Minnesota et al. v. Mille Lacs Band of Chippewa Indians et al.*

NATIVE AMERICAN LEGENDS OF THE GREAT LAKES AND THE MISSISSIPPI VALLEY

PART ONE

Earth · Flood · Fire

THE EARTH-MAKER

Winnebago

When Earth-maker came to consciousness, he thought of the substance upon which he was sitting. He saw nothing. There was nothing anywhere. Therefore his tears flowed. He wept. But not long did he think of it. He took some of the substance upon which he was sitting; so he made a little piece of earth for our fathers. He cast this down from the high place on which he sat. Then he looked at what he had made. It had become something like our earth. Nothing grew upon it. Bare it was, but not quiet. It kept turning.

"How shall I make it become quiet?" thought Earth-maker. Then he took some grass from the substance he was sitting upon and cast it down upon the earth. Yet it was not quiet.

Then he made a man. When he had finished him, he called him Tortoise. At the end of all his thinking, after he came to consciousness, he made the two-legged walkers.

Then Earth-maker said to this man, "The evil spirits are abroad to destroy all I have just created. Tortoise, I shall send you to bring order into the world." Then Earth-maker gave him a knife.

But when Tortoise came to earth, he began to make war. He did not look after Earth-maker's creation. So Earth-maker took him back.

Then he sent Hare down to earth to restore

order. He said, "See, Grandmother, I have done the work my father directed me to do. The lives of my uncles and aunts, the two-legged walkers, will be endless like mine."

His grandmother said, "Grandson, how could you make the lives of your uncles and aunts endless like yours? How could you do something in a way Earth-maker had not intended it to be? Earth-maker could not make them thus."

Hare thought, "My grandmother must be related to some of the evil spirits I have killed. She does not like what I have done, for she is saying that I killed the evil spirits."

Now Grandmother heard him think. "No, Grandson, I am not thinking of that. I am saying that our father made death so there should not be a lack of food on earth. He made death to prevent overcrowding. He also made a spirit world in which they should live after death."

Hare did not like what she said. "Grandmother surely does not like it," he thought. "She must be related to the evil spirits."

"No, Grandson, it is not so. But to quiet you, your uncle and aunts will live to be very old." Then she spoke again, "Now, Grandson, stand up. The two-legged walkers shall follow me always. I shall follow you always. Therefore try to do what I tell you. Remember you are a man. Do not look back after you have started."

Then they started to go around the earth.

"Do not look back," she said.

"I wonder why she says that," thought Hare. Then he turned his head the least little bit to the left, and looked back to the place from which they had started. Instantly everything caved in.

"Oh, my! Oh, my! exclaimed Grandmother. "Grandson, a man you are; but I thought you were a great man, so I greatly encouraged you. Now even if I wished to, I could not prevent death."

This she meant, so they say.

Then they went around the earth, to the edge of the fire which encircles the earth. That way they went, so they say.

CREATION

Chitimacha

There was a Creator of All Things. This Great Mystery understood all things. He had no eyes, yet he could see. He had no ears, yet he could hear. He had a body, but it could not be seen.

When the earth was first made, the Creator of All Things placed it under the water. The fish were first created. But when the Creator wanted to make men, there was no dry land. Therefore Crawfish was sent down to bring up a little earth. He brought up mud in his claws. Immediately it spread out and the earth appeared above the waters. Then the Great Mystery made men. He made the Chitimachas. It was at Natchez that he first made them.

He gave them laws, but the people did not follow the laws. Therefore many troubles came, so that the Creator could not rest. Therefore the Creator made tobacco. Then men could become quiet and rest. Afterwards he made women, but at first they were like wood. So he directed a chief to teach them how to move, and how to cook, and how to sew skins.

Now when the animals met the Chitimachas, they ridiculed them. For these men had no fur, and no wool, and no feathers to protect them from storms, or rain, or the hot sun. The Chitimachas were sad because of this.

Then the Creator gave them bows and arrows, and taught them how these things should be used. He told them that the flesh of the animals was good for food, and their skins for covering. Thus the animals were punished.

The Creator taught them also how to draw fire from two pieces of wood, one flat and the other pointed; thus they learned to cook their food. The Creator taught them also to honor the bones of their relatives; and so long as they lived, to bring them food.

Now in those days, the animals took part in the councils of men. They gave advice to men, being wiser. Each animal took especial care of the Chitimachas. Therefore the Indians respect the animals which gave good advice to their ancestors, and this aids them even today in time of need.

The Creator also made the moon and the stars. Both were to give life and light to all things on earth. Moon forgot the sacred bathing; therefore he is pale and weak, giving but little light to man. But Sun gives light to all things. Sun often stops on her trail to give more time to the Indians when they are hunting, or fighting their enemies. Moon does not, but always pursues his wife over the sky trail. Yet he can never catch up with her.

The mounds in the Chitimacha country are the camping places of the spirit sent down by the Creator to visit the Indians. This spirit taught the men how to cook their food and to cure their wounds. He is still highly honored.

THE CREATION

Wyandot

There was, in olden days, something the matter with the earth. It has changed. We think so. We think the Great Mystery made it and made men also. He made them at a place called Mountains. It was eastward. When he had made the earth and these mountains, he covered the earth over with something. He did it with his hands.

Under this, he put men. All the different tribes were there. One of the young men climbed up and found his way to the surface. It was very beautiful. Then a deer ran past, with an arrow in its side. He followed it to where it fell and died. He Looked back to see its tracks, and he soon saw other tracks. They were the footprints of the person who shot the deer. He soon came up. It was the Maker of Men. Thus he taught the Indians what they must do when they came out of the earth. The creator showed the Indian how to skin the deer, and prepare it for food, and how to use the skin for dress.

When everything was ready, he said, "Make a fire."

The Indian said, "I do not know how."

Therefore the creator made the fire. Then he said, "Put the meat on the fire. Roast it."

The Indian did this, but he did not turn the stick. Therefore it was burned on one side and not roasted on the other. So the creator showed him how to turn the stick.

Then the Great Mystery called all the Indians up out of the earth. They came out by tribes. To each tribe he gave a chief. Then he made a head chief over all the tribes, who should teach them what they should do.

The Great Mystery also made Good and Evil. They were brothers. One made pleasant things grow. The other spent all his time spoiling his brother's work. He made stony places, and rocks, and made bad fruits to grow. He made great trouble among men. He annoyed them very much. Good had to go back and do his work over again. It kept him very busy. Then Good decided to destroy Evil.

Therefore Good proposed to run a race with Evil. When they met, Good said, "Tell me first—what do you most fear?"

"Bucks' horns," said Evil. "What do you most fear?'

"Indian grass braided," said Good.

Then Evil at once went to his grandmother, who braided Indian grass. He got a great deal of it. He put the grass in the trail, and put it in the limbs of the trees along the trail where Good was to run. Good also filled the path, where his brother Evil was to run, with bucks' horns.

They said, "Who shall run first?" They argued about it. At last Good said, "Well, I will, because I proposed the race." So he started off and Evil followed him. When Good became tired, he pulled down a strand of braided green grass and chewed it. Thus he ran rapidly. But Evil became tired. Yet Good would not stop until he reached the end of the trail.

The next day Evil started on his trail. Everywhere he was stopped by the branches of bucks' horns. They greatly annoyed him. He said to Good, "Let me stop." Good said,

"No, you must go on." At last, towards evening, Evil fell in the trail. At once Good took bucks' horns and killed him.

Then Good returned to his grandmother. She was very angry. She loved Evil. That night Good was awakened by a sound. The spirit of Evil was talking with his grandmother. Then when Evil knew Good was awake, he said, "Let me into the wigwam." But Good always said, "No."

At last Evil said, "I go to the northwest land. You will never see me more. Those who follow me will never come back. Death will keep them."

CREATION OF THE RACES*

Biloxi

Kuti Mandkce, the One Above, made people. He made one person, an Indian. While the Indian was sleeping, he made a woman. The One Above went away to find food for the man and woman.

After he left, something was standing there upright. It was a tree. A person said, "Why do you not eat the fruit of this tree? I think he made it for you to eat."

So the woman pulled off some fruit and stewed it, and she and the Indian ate it. Shortly after, the One Above returned. Now he had gone away to find food for them. When he found they had stewed this fruit, he

* Obviously influenced by missionary teaching, but a most curious myth.

was very angry. He said, "Work for yourself. Find your own food, else you shall be hungry."

When the One Above had been a long time gone, he sent back a letter to the Indians. But the Indians did not receive it, because the Americans took it. That is why Americans know how to read and write.

Now after the letter came, the people found a very clear stream of water. The American found it first and lay down in it; therefore he is very white all over. Next came the Frenchman, but the water was not so clear. Then came the Indians; therefore Indians are not of light complexion, because they did not find the water when it was clear. Afterwards came the Spaniard, and he was not white, because the water had become very muddy.

Some time after the Negro was made. The One Above thought he should attend to work, so he made the Negro's nose flat. And by this time the water was very muddy, and the stream was very low. So the Negro washed only the palms of his hands. Therefore Negroes are very black except on the palms of their hands.

STORY OF THE CREATION

Ojibwa

When Gitche Manito, the Good Mystery, created the earth-plain, it was bare, without trees or shrubs. Then he created two Indians, a man and a woman. Now when there were ten persons on the earth-plain, death happened. The first man lamented, and went back and forth over the plain, complaining.

He said, "Why did the Good Spirit send death so soon?" The Good Mystery heard this. He called a great council. He said, "Man is not happy. I have made him very frail, therefore death happens. What shall we do?"

The council lasted six days, and there was not a breath of air to disturb the waters. The seventh was the *nageezhik,* the excellent day. The sky was blue and there were no clouds. On that day Gitche Manito sent down a messenger to earth. In his right hand was a piece of white hare's skin, and in the left the head of a white-headed eagle. On each was the blue stripe of peace.

The messenger said, "Gitche Manito sent me. He has heard your words. You must obey his commands." Then he gave to the Indians the hare's skin, the eagle's head, and a white otter skin with the blue stripe of peace.

Thus Gitche Manito taught the Indians how to make magic and how to be strong.

CREATION (a fragment)

Ojibwa

Long ago, Nokomis came down from Sky-land, but remained fluttering in midair. There was no place on which to rest her foot.

The Fishes at once held a great council. Now Tortoise had a shell-covered back, very broad. After the council, he rose to the surface so that Nokomis might rest upon his back. Then the drift-masses of the sea gathered about the Tortoise. Thus the land was made.

Then Nokomis found herself alone on the land. So she married a manito from the Sky-land. Two sons had Nokomis—twin brothers. But the brothers were not friends. One was a good huntsman; the other could kill no game at all. So they disputed. Then one brother rose to the Sky-land. He caused the Thunders to roar over his brother's head.

Now the sister of these twin brothers was the ancestor of the Ojibwas.

CREATION OF THE MANDANS

Mandan

The Mandans were the People of the Pheasants. They were the first people in the world. At first they lived in the earth. Now, in the dark Earth-land, they had many vines. Then at last one vine grew up through a hole in the Earth-plain, far above their heads. One of their young men at once went up the vine until he came out on the Earth-plain. He came out on the prairies, on the bank of a river, just where the Mandan village now stands.*

He looked all about him. The Earth-plain was very beautiful. There were many buffaloes there. He killed one with his bow and arrow, and found it was good for food.

Then the young men returned to his people under the ground. He told them all he had seen. They held a council, and then they began climb up the vine to the Earth-plain. Some of the chiefs, and the young warriors, and many of the women went up. Then came a very fat woman. The chiefs said, "Do not go up." But she did, so the vine broke.

The Mandans were very sorry about this. Because no more could go up, the tribe on the Earth-plain is not very large. And no one could return to his village in the ground. Therefore the Mandans built their village on the banks of the river. But the rest of the people remained underground.

* 1834.

THE FLOOD

Chitimacha

Long, long ago, a great storm came. At once the people baked a great earthen pot, and in this two of them saved themselves. The pot was held up on the surface of the water. Now two rattlesnakes were also saved in the earthen jar, because in the olden days rattlesnakes were the friends of man. In those days, when an Indian left his lodge the rattlesnake entered it and protected it until he returned.

When all the land was flooded, the red-headed woodpecker hooked his claws into the sky and so hung above the waters. But the flood rose so high that part of his tail was wet. You can see the marks even to this day.

When the waters sank, he was sent to find land. He could find none. Then a dove was sent and came back with a grain of sand. This sand was placed on top of the great waters and immediately it stretched out. It became dry land. Therefore the dove is called "Ground Watcher."

THE GREAT FLOOD (a fragment)

Mandan

The earth is a large tortoise. It moves very slowly and carries a great deal of earth on its back. Long ago there was a tribe which is now dead. They used to dig deep down in the earth for badgers. They dug with knives. One day they stuck a knife far down into the earth. It cut through the shell of Tortoise.

Therefore Tortoise at once began to sink into the water. The water rose through the knife cut until it covered all the ground. All the people were drowned except one man.

But some of the old people say it was this way. They say there were four Tortoises, one in the East, one in the West, one in the South, and another in the North. Each Tortoise made it rain for ten days. Therefore the water covered the earth and all the people were drowned.

THE GREAT FLOOD

Menomini

Manabush* wanted to punish the evil manitoes, the Ana maqkiu who had destroyed his brother Wolf. Therefore he invented the ball game.

The place selected by Manabush for a ball ground was near a large sand bar on a great lake near Mackinac. He asked the Thunderers to play against the Ana maqkiu. These evil manitoes came out of the ground as Bears. One chief was a silvery white bear, and the other a gray bear. They played the ball game all day. Manabush watched the game from a tree on a knoll.

When night came, Manabush went to a spot between the places where the Bear chiefs had played ball. He said, "I want to be a pine tree, cut off halfway between the ground and the top, with two strong branches reaching out over the places where the Bear chiefs lie down." At once he became just such a tree.

Now when the players came to the ball game the next morning, the Bear chiefs at once said, "This tree was not standing there yesterday."

The Thunderers at once said, "Oh, yes. It was there." Thus they argued. At last one Bear chief said, "This tree is Manabush. Therefore we will kill him." At once they

* The Manabozho of the Ojibwas.

sent for Grizzly Bear. They said, "Climb this tree. Tear off the bark. Scratch it." Grizzly Bear did so. He also bit the branches.

Then the Bear chiefs called to Serpent. They said, "Ho, Serpent! Come climb this tree. Bite it. Strangle it in your coils." Serpent at once did so. It was very hard for Manabush; yet he said nothing at all.

Then the Bear chiefs said, "No, it is not Manabush. Therefore we will finish the game."

Now when they were playing, someone carried the ball so far that the Bear chiefs were left entirely alone. At once Manabush drew an arrow from his quiver and shot the White Bear chief. Then he shot another arrow at Gray Bear chief. He wounded both of them. Then Manabush became a man again and ran for the sand bar. Soon the underground Ana maqkiu came back. They saw the two Bear chiefs were wounded. They immediately called for a flood from the earth to drown Manabush. It came very quickly and followed that one. Then Badger came. He hid Manabush in the earth. As he burrowed, he threw the earth behind him, and that held the water back. So the Ana maqkiu could not find Manabush. Therefore they gave up the search just as the water began to fill Badger's burrow. So Manabush and Badger returned above ground.

Now the underground people carried their chiefs to a wigwam. They said to an old woman, "Take care of them." Then Manabush followed them. He met the old woman. He took her skin and hid himself in it. So he went into the wigwam. He killed both the Bear chiefs. Then he took the skins of the bears. When he came out of the wigwam he shook a network of basswood twigs, so that the Ana maqkiu might know he had been there.

At once they pursued him. Water poured out of the earth in many places. A great flood came.

Manabush at once ran to the top of the highest mountain. The waters followed him closely. He climbed a great pine tree on the mountain top, but the waters soon reached him. Manabush said to the pine, "Grow twice as high." At once it did so. Yet the waters rose higher. Manabush said again to the tree, "Grow twice as high."

He said this four times, yet the waters kept rising until they reached his arm pits. Then Manabush called to Kisha Manido for help. The Good Mystery at once commanded the waters to stop.

Manabush looked around. There were only a few animals in the water. He called, "Ho, Otter! Come to me and be my brother. Dive down into the water. Bring up some earth that I may make a new world." Otter dived down into the water and was gone a long time. When he appeared again on the surface, Manabush saw he was drowned.

Then he called again, "Ho, Mink! Come to me and be my brother. Dive down into the water. Bring me some earth." Then Mink dived into the water. He was gone a long time. He also was drowned.

Manabush looked about him again. He saw Muskrat. He called, "Ho, Muskrat! Come to me and be my brother. Dive down into the water. Bring me up earth from below." Muskrat immediately dived into the water. He was gone a very long time. Then when he came up, Manabush went to him. In his paw was a tiny bit of mud. Then Manabush held Muskrat up, and blew on him, so he became alive again.

Then Manabush took the earth. He rubbed it between the palms of his hands and threw it out on the water. Thus a new world was made and trees appeared on it.

Manabush told Muskrat that his tribe should always be numerous, and the wherever his people should live they should have enough to eat.

Then Manabush found Badger. To him he gave the skin of the Gray Bear chief. But he kept for himself the skin of the silvery White Bear chief.

ORIGIN OF FIRE

Menomini

While Manabush was still a young man, he said to Nokomis, the Earth, "Grandmother, it is cold here and we have no fire. I shall go and get some."

Nokomis said, "Oh, no! It is too dangerous."

But Manabush said, "Yes, we must have fire."

At once Manabush made a canoe of birch bark. Then he became a rabbit. So he started eastward, across the great water, to a land where lived an old man who had fire. He guarded the fire carefully so that people might not steal it.

Now the old man had two daughters. One day they came out of the sacred wigwam where the fire was kept. Behold! There was a little rabbit, wet and cold and trembling. They took it up at once in their arms. They carried it into the wigwam. They set it down near the fire.

So Manabush sat by the fire while the two girls were busy. The old man was asleep. Then

Rabbit hopped nearer the fire. When he hopped, the whole earth shook. The old man roused. He said, "My daughters, what has happened?"

The girls answered, "Nothing at all. We picked up a little wet rabbit and are letting him dry by the fire." Then again the old man fell asleep. The girls were busy.

Suddenly Rabbit seized a stick of burning wood and ran out of the wigwam. He ran with great speed towards his canoe. The old man and the two girls followed him closely. But Rabbit reached his canoe and paddled quickly away, to the wigwam of Nokomis. He paddled so quickly that the fire stick burned fiercely. Sparks flew from it and burned Rabbit.

At once Rabbit and Nokomis gave fire to the Thunderers. They have had the care of fire ever since.

THE THUNDERERS AND THE ORIGIN OF FIRE

Menomini

When the Great Mystery created the earth, he made also many manitoes. Those of animal form were People of the Underground, and evil. But the bird manitoes were Eagles and Hawks. They were the Thunderers. The golden eagle was the Thunder-which-no-one-could-see.

Now when Masha Manido, the Good Mystery, saw that Bear was still an animal, he permitted him to change his form. Thus Bear became an Indian, with light skin. All this happened near Menomini River, near where it empties into Green Bay. At this place also Bear first came out of the ground.

Bear found himself alone, so he called to Eagle, "Ho, Eagle! Come to me and be my brother." So Eagle came down to earth and became an Indian.

While the Thunderers stood there, Beaver came near. Now as Beaver was a woman, she became a younger brother of the Thunderers. Soon after, as Bear and Eagle stood on a river bank, they saw a stranger, Sturgeon. They called to him. Therefore Sturgeon became Bear's younger brother and his servant. So also Elk was adopted by the Thunderers. He became a younger brother and water carrier.

At another time, Bear was going up Wisconsin River and sat down to rest. Out from beneath a waterfall came Wolf.

Wolf said, "What are you doing in this place?"

Bear said, "I am traveling to the source of the river. I am resting."

Just then Crane came flying by. Bear called, "Ho, Crane. Carry me to my people at the head of the river. Then will I make you my younger brother."

Crane stopped and took Bear on his back. As he was flying off, Wolf called, "Ho, Bear. Take me also as your younger brother. I am alone."

Bear said, "I will take Wolf as my younger brother."

This is how Wolf and Crane became younger brothers of Bear. Wolf afterwards let Dog and Deer join him, having seats in the council.

Now Big Thunder lived at Winnebago Lake, near Fond du Lac. The Thunderers were all made by Masha Manido to be of benefit to the whole world. When they return from the Southwest in the spring, they bring with them the rains which make the earth green and the plants and trees to grow. It if were not for the Thunderers, the earth would be dry and all things would perish.

Masha Manido gave to the Thunderers squaw corn, which grows on small sticks and has ears of several colors.

The Thunderers were also the Makers-of-Fire. Manabush first gave it to them, but he had stolen it from an old man living on an island in the middle of a great lake.

Bear and Sturgeon owned rice, which grew abundantly in the waters near Bear's village. One day the Thunderers visited Bear's village and promised to give corn and fire, if Bear would give them rice.

The Thunderers are the war chiefs and have charge of the lighting of the fire. So Bear gave rice to them. Then he built a long tepee and a fire was kindled in the center by the Thunderers. From this all the people of the earth received fire. It was carried to them by the Thunderers. When the people travel, the Thunderers go ahead to the camping place and start the fire which is used by all.

THE ORIGIN OF FIRE

Chitimacha

Fire first came from the Great Being, Kutnakin. He gave it into the care of an Indian so old that he was blind.

Now the Indians all knew that fire was good, therefore they tried to steal it. The old man could not see them when they came stealthily to his wigwam, but he could feel the presence of anyone. Then he would beat about him with his stick until he drove away the seekers for fire.

Now one day an Indian seized the fire suddenly. At once the Watcher of the Fire began beating about him with his stick, until the thief dropped the fire. But the old man did not know he had dropped it. He still beat about him so fiercely with his stick that he pounded some of the fire into a log.

That is why fire is in wood.

THE GIFTS OF THE SKY GOD

Chitimacha

Long, long ago, many Indians started to reach the Sky-world. They walked far to the north until they came to the edge of the sky, where it is fitted down over the Earth-plain. When they came to this place, they tried to slip through a crack under the edge, but the Sky-cover came down very tightly and quickly, and crushed all but six. These six had slipped through into the Sky-land.

Then these men began to climb up, walking far over the sky floor. At last they came to the lodge of Kutnakin. They stayed with him as his guests. At last they wished to go back to their own lodges on the Earth-plain.

Kutnakin said, "How will you go down to the Earth-plain?"

One said, "I will go down as a squirrel." So he started to spring down from the Sky-land. He was dashed to pieces.

Kutnakin said to the next, "How will you go down to the Earth-plain?"

And this man also went as an animal. And so the next one also. They were dashed to pieces. Then the others saw that they were crushed by their fall.

Therefore the fourth said, "I will go down as a spider." And he spun a long line down which he climbed safely to earth.

The fifth said, "I will go down as an eagle,"

and he spread his wings and circled through the air until he alighted on a tree branch.

The last one said, "I will go down as a pigeon," and so he came softly to earth.

Now each one brought back a gift from Kutnakin. The one who came back as a spider had learned how to howl and sing and dance when people were sick. He was the first medicine man. But one Indian had died while these six men were up in the Sky-land. He died before the shaman came down to earth as a spider. Therefore death came among the Indians. Had the shaman come back to earth in time to heal this Indian, there would have been no death.

The one who came back as an eagle taught men how to fish. And the pigeon taught the Indians the use of wild maize.

PART TWO

Corn · Wind · Thunder

MONDAMIN

Ojibwa

When the springtime came, long, long ago, an Indian boy began his fast, according to the customs of his tribe. His father was a very good man but he was not a good hunter, and often there was no food in the wigwam.

So, as the boy wandered from his small tepee in the forest, he thought about these things. He looked at the plants and shrubs and wondered about their uses, and whether they were good for food. He thought, "I must find out about these things in my vision."

One day, as he lay stretched upon his bed of robes in the solitary wigwam, a handsome Indian youth came down from Sky-land. He was gaily dressed in robes of green and yellow, with a plume of waving feathers in his hands.

"I am sent to you," said the stranger, "by the Great Mystery. He will teach you what you would know." Then he told the boy to rise and wrestle with him. The boy at once did so. At last the visitor said, "That is enough. I will come tomorrow."

The next day the beautiful stranger came again from the Sky-land. Again the two wrestled until the stranger said, "That is enough. I will come tomorrow."

The third day he came again. Again the fasting youth found his strength increase as he wrestled with the visitor. Then that one said,

"It is enough. You have conquered." He sat himself down in the wigwam. "The Great Mystery has granted your wish," he said. "Tomorrow when I come, after we have wrestled and you have thrown me down, you must strip off my garments. Clear the earth of roots and weeds and bury my body. Then leave this place; but come often and keep the earth soft, and pull up the weeds. Let no grass or weeds grow on my grave." Then he went away, but first he said, "Touch no food until after we wrestle tomorrow."

The next morning the father brought food to his son; it was the seventh day of fasting. But the boy refused until the evening should come.

Again came the handsome youth from the Sky-land. They wrestled long, until he fell to the earth. Then the Indian boy took off the green and yellow robes, and buried his friend in soft, fresh earth. Thus the vision had come to him.

Then the boy returned to his father's lodge, for his fasting was ended. Yet he remembered the commands of the Sky-land stranger. Often he visited the grave, keeping it soft and fresh, pulling up weeds and grass. And when people were saying that the Summer-maker would soon go away and the Winter-maker come, the boy went with his father to the place where his wigwam had stood in the forest while he fasted. There they found a tall and graceful plant, with bright silky hair, and green and yellow robes.

"It is Mondamin," said the boy. "It is Mondamin, the corn."*

* Then Nokomis, the old woman,
Spake, and said to Minnehaha:
"'Tis the Moon when leaves are falling;
All the wild rice has been gathered,
And the maize is ripe and ready;
Let us gather in the harvest,
Let us wrestle with Mondamin,
Strip him of his plumes and tassels,
Of his garments green and yellow."

—*Hiawatha*

MONDAMIN

Ottawa

When the Ottawas lived on the Manatoline Islands, in Lake Huron, they had a very strong medicine man. His name was Mass-wa-wei-nini, Living Statue. Then the Iroquois came and drove the Ottawas away. They fled to Lac Court Oreilles, between Lake Superior and the Mississippi River. But Living Statue remained in the land of his people. He remained to watch the Iroquois, so that his people might know of their plans. His two sons stayed with him.

At night, the medicine man paddled softly around the island, in his canoe. He paddled through the water around the beautiful green island of his people. One morning he rose early to go hunting. His two boys were asleep. So Living Statue followed the game trail through the forest; then he came to a wide green plain. He watched keenly for the enemy of his people. Then he began to cross the plain.

When Living Statue was in the middle of the plain, he saw a small man coming towards him. He wore a red plume in his hair.

"Where are you going?" asked Red Plume.

"I am hunting," said Living Statue.

Red Plume drew out his pipe and they smoked together.

"Where does your strength come from?" asked Red Plume.

"I have the strength common to all men," said Living Statue.

"We must wrestle," said Red Plume. "If you can make me fall, you will cry, 'I have thrown you, *Wa ge me na!*'"

Now when they had finished smoking, they began to wrestle. They struggled long. Red Plume was small, but his medicine was strong. Living Statue grew weaker and weaker, but at last, by a sudden effort, he threw Red Plume. At once he cried, "I have thrown you, *Wa ge me na!*"

Immediately Red Plume vanished. When Living Statue looked at the place where he had fallen, he saw only *Mondamin,* an ear of corn. It was crooked. There was a red tassel at the top.

Someone said, "Take off my robes. Pull me in pieces. Throw me over the plain. Take the spine on which I grew and throw it in shady places near the edge of the wood. Return after one moon. Tell no one."

Mass-wa-wei-nini did as the voice directed. Then he returned into the woods. He killed a deer. So he returned to his wigwam.

Now after one moon, he returned to the plain. Behold! There were blades and spikes of young corn. And from the broken bits of spine, grew long pumpkin vines.

When summer was gone, Living Statue went again to the plain with his sons. The corn was in full ear. Also the large pumpkins were ripe.

Thus the Ottawas received the gift of corn.

THE CORN WOMAN

Cherokee

One day a hunter could find no game. He had but a few grains of corn with him. He was very hungry. In the night a dream came to him and he heard the sound of singing.

Early the next morning the hunter rose, but again he found no game. When he slept again the dream came to him, and again came the sound of singing, but this time it was nearer. Yet again he could find no game.

The third night the dream came to the hunter, and when he awoke, he still heard the song. Then he rose quickly and followed the song. At last he came to a single green stalk of Selu.

The stalk spoke to him. It said, "Take off my roots, and take them with you to your wigwam. Tomorrow morning you must chew them before anyone awakes. Then go again into the woods. So will you always be successful in hunting."

The green stalk gave him many directions for hunting the elk and the deer. So it talked until the sun rose to the very top of the sky trail. Immediately the green stalk became a woman. She rose gracefully into the air and vanished.

Then all the people knew that the hunter had seen Selu, the Corn, wife of Kanati. Therefore the hunter was always successful.

DISCOVERY OF THE WILD RICE

Ojibwa

Long ago, Wenibojó* made his home with his grandmother, Nokomis. One day Nokomis said to her grandson, "Prove yourself a man. Take a long journey. Go through the great forests. Fast you. Prepare for the hardships of life."

So Wenibojó took his bow and arrow from his wigwam. He wandered out into the forest. Many days he wandered. Then at last he reached a broad lake, covered thick with heavy-headed stalks. But Wenibojó knew not that the grain was food.

So Wenibojó went back to his grandmother, Nokomis. He told her of the broad, quiet lake, with the heavy-headed stalks. So Nokomis came, and in their canoe they gathered the wild rice and sowed it in another lake.

Again Wenibojó left Nokomis. With his bow and arrow he wandered far into the forest. Then some little bushes spoke as he walked. "Sometimes they eat us," they said. Wenibojó made no answer. Again the bushes spoke, "Sometimes they eat us."

"Who are you talking to," he asked.

"To Wenibojó," they said. So he bent down and dug up the bushes by the roots. The roots were long, like an arrow. They

* Another form of the Ojibwa Manabozho, or the Menomini Manabush.

were good to eat, but Wenibojó had fasted too long.

After a while, Wenibojó wandered on. He was very hungry. Many bushes spoke to him. Many said, "Sometimes they eat us," but he made no answer.

One day he followed the river trail, when the sun was high. Many little bunches of straw were growing out of the water. They spoke to him. They said, "Wenibojó, sometimes they eat us."

So Wenibojó picked some of the grains from the heavy-headed stalks and ate.

"You are good to eat," he said. "What do they call you?"

"They call us *manomin,*" answered the wild rice.

Then Wenibojó waded far out into the water. He beat out grains and ate many. They were good for food.

Then Wenibojó remembered the grain which Nokomis had sown, and he returned to his grandmother and the *manomin* lake.

ORIGIN OF WILD RICE

Ojibwa

Now one evening Wenibojó returned to his wigwam from hunting. He had found no game. As he came towards his fire, he saw a duck sitting on the edge of a kettle of boiling water. Immediately the duck flew away.

Wenibojó looked in the kettle. Behold! Grains were floating upon the water. Then he ate the broth made with the grains. It was good.

So Wenibojó followed the trail of the duck. He came to a lake of *manomin.* All the birds and the ducks and geese were eating the grain. Therefore Wenibojó learned to know *manomin,* the wild rice.

ORIGIN OF WINNEBAGO

Menomini

One day Manabush walked along the lake shore. He was tired and hungry. Then he saw, around a sand spit jutting far out into the water, many waterfowl.

Now Manabush had with him only a medicine bag. He hung that on a manabush tree in the brush. He put a roll of bark on his back, and returned to the lake shore. He passed slowly by so as not to frighten the birds. Duck and Swan suddenly recognized him, and swam quickly away from the shore.

One of the Swans called out, "Ho! Manabush, where are you going?"

"I am going to have a dance," said Manabush. "As you may see, I have all my songs with me."

Then he called out to all the birds, "Come to me, brothers! Let us sing and dance."

At once the birds returned to the shore and walked back upon an open space in the grass. Manabush took the bundle of bark from his back. He placed it on the ground, got out his singing sticks, and then he said to the birds, "Now all of you dance around me as I drum. Sing as loudly as you can and keep your eyes closed. The first to look will always have red eyes."

So Manabush began to beat time upon his bundle of bark. The birds with eyes closed danced around him. Then Manabush began to keep time with one hand, as the birds sang loudly. With the other he seized a Swan by the neck. Swan gave a loud squawk.

"That's right, brothers! Sing as loudly as you can," shouted Manabush.

Soon he seized another Swan by the neck. Then he seized a Goose. At last there were not so many birds singing. Then a tiny duck opened his eyes to see why. At once he shrieked, "Manabush is killing us! Manabush is killing us!" And he started for the water, followed by the rest of the birds.

Now this little duck was a poor runner. Manabush quickly caught him and said, "I won't kill you; but you shall always have red eyes. And you shall be the laughingstock of all the birds."

And with that Manabush pushed him so hard, yet holding on to his tail, that the duck went far out into the middle of the lake and his tail came off. Because of that he has red eyes and no tail, even to this day.

Then Manabush gathered up the birds he had killed and took them out on the sand spit. He buried them in the sand and built a fire over them to cook them, but he left sticking out the heads of some and the legs of others so he would know where they were.

But Manabush was tired. He slapped his thigh and said, "You watch the birds and awaken me if anyone comes near them." He stretched out on the sand with his back to the fire and went to sleep.

After a while, Indians came along in their canoes. They saw the fire and the roasting birds. They went ashore on the sand spit. They pulled out the birds and ate them. But they put back into the sand the heads and feet, just as they had found them. So they departed.

Afterwards, Manabush awoke, very hungry. He pulled at the head of a swan. Behold! The head came out, but there was no bird. He pulled at the feet of a goose. No bird was there. So he tried every head and foot; but the birds were gone.

He slapped his thigh again and asked, "Who has been here? Someone has robbed me of my feast. I told you to watch."

His thigh answered, "I fell asleep also. I was very tired. See! There are people moving away in their canoes! They are dirty and poorly dressed." Then Manabush ran to the point of the sand spit. He could see the people who were just disappearing around a point. He shouted, "Winnebago! Winnebago!" Therefore the Menomini have always called their thievish neighbors Winnebago.

THE ORIGIN OF TOBACCO

Menomini

One day when Manabush was passing by a high mountain, a fragrant odor came to him from a crevice in the cliffs. He went closer. Then he knew that in the mountain was a giant who was the Keeper of the Tobacco. He entered the mouth of a cave, going through a long tunnel to the center of the mountain.

There in a great wigwam was the giant. The giant said sternly, "What do you want?"

Manabush said, "I want some tobacco."

"Come back again in one year," said the giant. "The manitoes have just been here for their smoke. They come but once a year."

Manabush looked around. He saw a great number of bags filled with tobacco. He seized one and ran out into the open air, and close after him came the giant.

Up to the mountain tops fled Manabush, leaping from peak to peak. The giant came close behind him, springing with great bounds. When Manabush reached a very high peak, he suddenly lay flat on the ground; but the giant, leaping, went over him and fell into the chasm beyond.

The giant picked himself up, and began to climb up the face of the cliff. He almost reached the top, hanging to it by his hands. Manabush seized him, and drew him upwards, and dropped him down on the ground.

He said, "For your meanness, you shall become Kakuene, the jumper. You shall become the pest of those who raise tobacco." Thus the giant became a grasshopper.

Then Manabush took the tobacco, and divided it amongst his brothers, giving to each some of the seed. Therefore the Indians are never without tobacco.

ORIGIN OF MAPLE SUGAR

Menomini

One day Manabush returned from the hunt without any food. He could find no game at all. So Nokomis gathered all their robes, and the beaded belts, and their belongings together. They built a new wigwam among the sugar maple trees.

Nokomis said, "Grandson, go into the woods and gather for me pieces of birch bark. I am going to make sugar." Manabush went into the woods. He gathered strips of birch bark, which he took back to the wigwam. Nokomis had cut tiny strips of the bark to use as thread in sewing the bark into hollow buckets. Then Nokomis went from tree to tree cutting small holes through the maple bark, so that the sap might flow. She placed a birchbark vessel under each hole. Manabush followed her from tree to tree looking for the sap to drop. None fell. When Nokomis had finished, Manabush found all the vessels half full.

He stuck his finger into the thick syrup. It was sweet. Then he said, "Grandmother, this is all very good, but it will not do. If people make sugar so easily, they will not have to work at all. I will change all this. They must cut wood and keep the sap boiling several nights. Otherwise they will not be busy."

So Manabush climbed to the very top of a

tree. He showered water all over the maples, like rain. Therefore the sugar in the tree dissolved and flows from the tree as thin sap. This is why the uncles of Manabush and their children always have to work hard when they want to make sugar.

MANABUSH AND THE MOOSE

Menomini

Manabush killed a moose. He was very hungry, but he was greatly troubled as to how he should eat it.

"If I begin at the head," he said, "they will say I ate him headfirst. But if I begin at the side, they will say I ate him sideways. And if I begin at the tail, they will say I ate him tail first."

He was greatly troubled. And while he thus spoke, the wind blew two tree branches together. It made a harsh, creaking sound.

"I cannot eat in this noise," said Manabush, and he climbed the tree. Immediately the branches caught him by the arm and held him. Then a pack of wolves came and ate up the moose.

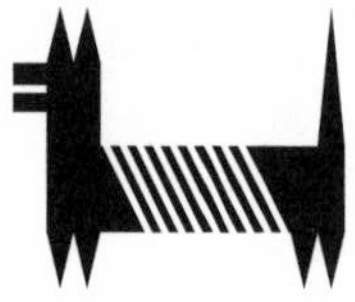

ORIGIN OF DAY AND NIGHT

Menomini

One day as Wabus, the Rabbit, traveled through a forest, he came to a clearing on the bank of the river. There sat Totoba, the Saw-whet Owl. The light was dim and Rabbit could not see well. He said to Saw-whet, "Why do you want it so dark? I do not like it. I will cause it to be light."

Saw-whet said, "Do so, if you are strong enough. Let us try our powers."

So Rabbit and the Owl called a great council of the birds. Some of the birds and animals wanted Rabbit to succeed so that it would be light. Others wanted it to remain dark.

Rabbit and Owl began to try their powers. Rabbit began to repeat rapidly, *"Wabon, Wabon, Wabon"* (Light, Light, Light), while Owl kept saying as rapidly as he could, *"Uni tipa qkot, Uni tipa qkot, Uni tipa qkot"* (Night, Night, Night).

If one of them should speak the word of the other, he would lose. So Rabbit kept repeating rapidly, *"Wabon, Wabon, Wabon,"* while Owl said as rapidly as he could, *"Uni tipa qkot, Uni tipa qkot, Uni tipa qkot."* At last Owl said Rabbit's word, *"Wabon,"* so he lost.

Therefore Rabbit decided there should be light. But because some of the animals and birds could hunt only in the dark, he said it should be night part of the time. But all the rest of the time it is day.

ORIGIN OF THE BEAR

Cherokee

Long ago, before the white man came, in the land of the Cherokees was a clan called the Ani Tsagulin. One of the boys of the clan used to wander all day long in the mountains. He never ate his food at home.

"Why do you do so?" asked his father and mother. The boy did not answer.

"Why do you do so?" they asked many days, as the boy wandered away into the hills. He did not answer them.

Then his mother saw that long brown hair covered his body. They said again, "Where do you go?" They asked, "Why do you not eat at home?"

At last the boy said, "There is plenty to eat there. It is better than the corn in the village. Soon I shall stay in the woods all the time."

His father and mother said, "No."

The boy kept saying, "It is better than here. I am beginning to be different. Soon I shall not want to live here. If you come with me you will not have to hunt, or to plant corn. But first you must fast seven days."

The people began to talk about it. They said, "Often we do not have enough to eat here. There he says there is plenty. We will go with him."

So they fasted seven days. Then they left their village and went to the mountains.

Now the other tribes had heard what they had talked in their village. At once they sent messengers. But when the messengers met them, they had started towards the mountains and their hair was long and brown. Their nature was changing. This was because they had fasted seven days. But the Ani Tsagulin would not go back to their village. They said to the others: "We are going where there is always plenty to eat. Hereafter we shall be called *Yana,* bears. When you are hungry, come into the woods and call us, and we will give you food to eat."

So they taught these messengers how to call them and to hunt them. Because, even though they may seem to be killed, the Ani Tsagulin live forever.

ORIGIN OF THE WORD CHICAGO

Ojibwa

Once an Ottawa hunter and his wife lived on the shores of Lake Michigan. Then the hunter went south, toward the end of the lake, to hunt. When he reached the lake* where he had caught beaver the year before, it was still covered with ice. Then he tapped the ice to find the thinner places where the beaver families lived. He broke holes at these weaker points in the ice, and went to his wigwam to get his traps.

* Between Milwaukee and Chicago, going south to where Chicago now stands.

Now the hunter's wife chanced to pass one of these holes and she saw a beaver on the ice. She caught it by the tail and called to the hunter to come and kill it quickly, before it could get back into the water.

"No," said the hunter, "if I kill this beaver, the others will become frightened. They will escape from the lake by other openings in the ice."

Then the woman became angry, and they quarreled.

When the sun was near setting, the hunter went out on the ice again, to set more traps. When he returned to his tepee, his wife had gone. He thought she had gone to make a visit. The next morning she had not returned, and he saw her footprints. So he followed her trail to the south. As he followed her trail, he saw that the footprints gradually changed. At last they became the trail of a skunk. The trail ended in a marsh, and many skunks were in that marsh.

Then he returned to his people. And he called the place, "The Place of the Skunk."

ORIGIN OF THE WORD CHICAGO*

Menomini

Potawatomi Indians used to live in the marshes where Chicago now stands. They sent out word to the other tribes that hunting was good. Then the Menomini Indians went to the marshes for game. In the night their dogs barked much. But when the Menomini Indians reached the spot where the dogs barked, they found only skunks.

* Schoolcraft gives the origin of the word Chicago, as follows:
Chi-cag The animal of the leek or wild onion.
Chi-cag-o-wunz The wild leek or polecat plant.
Chi-ca-go Place of the wild leek.
It would really seem, from the myths and the origin of the word, as given above, that the name originated from the great amount of skunk weed on the marshes now covered by the city.

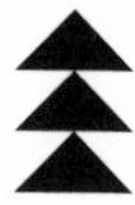

THE COMING OF MANABUSH

Menomini

When the daughter of Nokomis, the Earth, died, Nokomis wrapped her new baby in soft dry grass. She laid him on the ground under a large wooden bowl. Then she mourned four days for her daughter.

At the end of four days, Nokomis heard a sound in her wigwam. It came from the wooden bowl. Then she remembered. She took up the bowl. At once she saw a tiny white rabbit, with trembling pink ears. She took it up. She said, "Oh, my dear little Rabbit. Oh, my Manabush." She took care of him.

One day Rabbit hopped across the wigwam. The earth shook. At once the evil underground spirits, the Ana maqkiu, said to one another, "What has happened? A great manito is born somewhere!" Immediately they began to plot against him.

In this way Manabush came to earth. He soon grew to be a young man.

THE STORY OF MANABUSH*

Menomini

The daughter of Nokomis, the Earth, is the mother of Manabush, who is also the Fire. Flint first grew up out of Nokomis, and was alone. Then Flint made a bowl and filled it with earth. Wabus, the Rabbit, came from the earth, and became a man. Thus was Manabush created.

Beneath the earth lived the Underground People, the enemies of Manabush. They were the Ana maqkiu, who annoyed him constantly and sought to destroy him.

Now Manabush shaped a piece of flint to make an axe. While he was rubbing it on a rock, he heard the rock make sounds:

Ke ka ke ka ke ka ke ka

Goss goss goss goss

He soon understood what the rock was saying: that he was alone on the earth. That he had neither father, mother, brother, nor sister. This is what Flint said while Manabush was rubbing it upon the rock.

While he was thinking of this, he heard something coming. It was Mokquai, the Wolf. He said to Manabush, "Now you have a brother, for I, too, am alone. We shall live together and I will hunt for you."

* The Manabozho of the Ojibwa given by Longfellow as Hiawatha.

Manabush said, "I am glad to see you, my brother. Therefore I shall make you like myself." So he made him a man.

Then Manabush and his brother moved away to the shore of a lake and there built a wigwam. Manabush told his brother of the evil spirits, the Underground People, who lived beneath the water. He said, "Never go into the water, and never cross on the ice."

Now one day Wolf-brother went a-hunting. It was late when he started back. He found himself on the shore of the lake, just opposite the wigwam. He could see it clearly. He did not want to make a long journey around by the lake shore; therefore he began to cross on the ice. When he reached the middle of the lake, the ice broke. The Underground People pulled him under the water and he was drowned.

Now Manabush knew this. He mourned four days for Wolf-brother. On the fifth day, while he was following the hunting trail, he saw him approaching.

Wolf-brother said, "My fate will be the fate of all our people. They will all die, but after four days they will return." Then Manabush saw it was only the shade of his brother.

Then he said, "My brother, return to the place of the setting sun. You are now called Naqpote. You will have charge of the dead."

The Wolf-shade said, "If I go there, and others follow me, we shall not be able to return when we leave this place."

Manabush again spoke. He said, "Go, Naqpote. Prepare a wigwam for others. Build a large fire that they may be guided to it. When they arrive there must be a wigwam for them."

Thus Naqpote left the earth. He lives in the land of the shades, in the country of the setting sun, where the earth is cut off.

MANABOZHO AND WEST

Ojibwa

Manabozho lived with his grandmother Nokomis, the Earth, on the edge of a wide prairie. The first sound he heard was that of an owl. He quickly climbed down the tree. He ran to Nokomis.

"Noko," he cried, "I have heard a manito."

Nokomis said, "What kind of a noise did it make?"

"It said, *Ko ho, Ko ho!*" said Manabozho.

"Oh, it is only a bird," said Nokomis.

One day Manabozho thought, "It is very strange I know so little and grandmother is so wise. I wonder if I have any father or mother." He went back to the wigwam. He was very silent.

"What is the matter?" said Nokomis.

Manabozho asked, "Have I no father or mother?"

Now his mother had died when he was a very little baby, but Nokomis did not want to tell him. At last she said, "West is your father. He has three brothers. They are North, East, and South. They have great power. They travel on mighty wings. Your mother is not alive."

Manabozho said, "I will visit my father," but he meant to make war on him because he had learned that his father had not been kind to his mother and he meant to punish him.

Manabozho started on his journey. He traveled very rapidly. He went very far at each step. So at last he met his father, West, on the top of a high mountain. West was glad to see his son. Manabozho pretended to be glad.

They talked much. One day the son asked, "What are you most afraid of on earth?"

"Nothing," said West.

Manabozho said, "Oh, yes, there must be something."

At last West said, "There is a black stone on earth. I am afraid of that. If it should strike me, it would injure me." West said this was a great secret.

One day he asked Manabozho, "What are you most afraid of?"

"Nothing," was the answer.

"Oh, yes, there must be something you are afraid of," said West.

The son said, "*Ie-ee Ie-ee*—it is—it is—." He seemed afraid to mention it.

West said, "Don't be afraid!" Then at last his son said, "It is the root of the *apukwa,* the bulrush."

They quarreled because West had not been kind to the mother of Manabozho.

Some days later they quarreled. Manabozho said, "I will get some of the black rock."

"Oh no! Do not do so," cried West.

"Oh yes!" said his son.

West said at once, "I will get some of the *apukwa* root."

"Oh no!" cried Manabozho, pretending to be afraid. "Do not! Do not!"

"Oh, yes!" said West.

Manabozho at once went out and brought to his father's wigwam a large piece of black rock. West pulled up and brought in some bulrush roots. Manabozho threw the black rock at West. It broke in pieces. Therefore you may see pieces lying around even to this day. West struck his son with the bulrush root. Thus they fought. But at last Manabozho drove West far over the plains to the Darkening Land. So West came to the edge of the world, where the earth is broken off short. Then he cried, "Stop, my son! I am immortal, therefore I cannot be killed. I will remain here on the edge of the Earth-plain. You must go about doing good. You must kill monsters and serpents and all evil things. All the kingdoms of the earth are divided, but at the last you may sit with my brother North."*

Thus Manabozho became the Northwest wind.

* Back retreated Mudjekeewis
Rushing westward o'er the mountains,
Stumbling westward down the mountains,
Three whole days retreated fighting,
Still pursued by Hiawatha
To the doorways of the West-Wind,
To the portals of the Sunset . . .
. . . .
"Hold," at length cried Mudjekeewis,
"Hold, my son, my Hiawatha!
"'Tis impossible to kill me,
For you cannot kill the immortal."

—*Hiawatha*

MANABUSH AND THE GREAT FISH

Menomini *

After his brother Wolf had died, Manabush looked about him. He found he was no longer alone on earth. There were many other people, the children of Nokomis. They were his aunts and uncles.

The evil manitoes annoyed the people very much. Therefore Manabush wished to destroy them. Therefore he went to the shores of the lake where they lived. He called to the waters to disappear. Four times he called out. At once the waters vanished. There lay the Ana maqkiu. They lay on the mud in the bottom of the lake. They looked like fishes. The chief lay near the shore. He was very large.

Manabush said to Great Fish, "I shall destroy you because you will not allow my people to come near the shore." So he went towards Great Fish. But the smaller manitoes caused the waters to return. Thus they all escaped.

Then Manabush went into the woods. He made a canoe of birch bark. He wanted to destroy Great Fish in the water. As he left the shore in his canoe, he began to sing, "Great Fish, come and swallow me." Only the young fish came near. Manabush said scornfully, "I do not wish you. I want your chief to come and swallow me." Great Fish was much annoyed. He darted forward and swallowed Manabush and his canoe.

* The Ojibwas have a similar myth.

Thus Manabush found himself in the Great Fish. He looked about him. Many of his people were there. Bear and Deer, Porcupine and Raven, Buffalo, Pinetree Squirrel, and many others.

Manabush said to Buffalo, "My uncle, how did you get here? I never saw you near the water, but always on the prairie."

Buffalo said, "I came near the lake to get some fresh green grass. Great Fish caught me." And thus said all the animals. They said, "We came near the lake and Great Fish swallowed us."

Then Manabush said, "We will now have to go to the shore of Nokomis, my grandmother. You will all have to help me." At once they all began to dance around inside of Great Fish. Therefore he began to swim quickly towards shore. Manabush began to cut a hole over his head, so they could get out when Great Fish reached the shore of Nokomis, the Earth. They sang a magic song. They sang, "I see the sky. I see the sky." Pinetree Squirrel had a curious voice. He hopped around singing, *"Sek-sek-sek-sek!"* This was very amusing to the other people.

Great Fish thought, "I ought not to have swallowed that man. I must swim to the shore where Nokomis lives." So he swam quickly until he reached the beach. Then Manabush cut a larger hole. Thus they all climbed out of Great Fish. The birds helped Manabush. They stood on the sides of Great Fish and picked the flesh from his bones.*

* And again the sturgeon, Nahma,
Heard the shout of Hiawatha,
Heard his challenge of defiance,
The unnecessary tumult,
Ringing far across the water.
. . . .
In his wrath he darted upward,
Flashing leaped into the sunshine,
Opened his great jaws and swallowed
Both canoe and Hiawatha.

—*Hiawatha*

THE DEPARTURE OF MANABUSH

Menomini

Now Manabush was going away. He went to Mackinac. When he reached there, he made a high, narrow rock, and this he leaned against the cliff. This rock is as high as an arrow can be shot from a bow. At this place he was seen by his people for the last time. Before he went, he talked with them.

Manabush said, "I am going away now. I have been badly treated by other people who live in the land about you. I shall go across a great water towards the rising sun, where there is a land of rocks. There I shall set up my wigwam. When you hold a *mita-wiko-nik* and are all together, you shall think of me. When you speak my name, I shall hear you. Whatever you ask, that I will do."

Then Manabush spoke no more to his people. He entered the canoe. Then he went slowly over the great water, to the land of rocks. He vanished from his people as he went towards the rising sun.*

* The Ojibwas say he went toward the setting sun.
Thus departed Hiawatha,
Hiawatha the Beloved,
In the glory of the sunset,
In the purple mists of evening,
to the regions of the home-wind,
Of the Northwest wind, Keewaydin . . .

—*Hiawatha*

THE RETURN OF MANABUSH

Menomini

The uncles of Manabush, the people, used to visit a rock near Mackinac where the old men said Manabush was living. They built a long lodge there. They sang in their *mita-wiko-nik* there. Manabush heard them. Sometimes he came to them. He appeared as a little white rabbit, trembling, with pink ears, just as he had first appeared to Nokomis, his grandmother.

THE REQUEST FOR IMMORTALITY

Menomini

One day long after Manabush had gone away from his people, an Indian dreamed that he spoke to him. At daylight, he sought seven friends, chief men of the Mita-wit. They held a council together, and then rose and went in search of Manabush.

The Dreamer blackened his face.

On the shore of the Great Waters, they entered canoes, and paddled toward a rocky place in the Land of the Rising Sun. Very long they paddled over the water, until they reached the land where dwelt Manabush.

Soon they reached his wigwam. Manabush bade them enter. The door of the wigwam lifted and fell again as each one entered. When all were seated, Manabush said: "My friends, why is it you have come so long a journey to see me? What is it you wish?"

All but one answered, at once: "Manabush, we wish some hunting medicine; thus we may supply our people with much food."

"You shall have it," said Manabush. Then he turned to the silent one. He asked, "What do you wish?"

The Indian replied, "I wish no hunting medicine. I wish to live forever."

Manabush rose and went towards the Indian. He took him by the shoulders and carried him to his sleeping place. He set him down, and said: "You shall be a stone. Thus you shall be everlasting."

Immediately the other Indians arose and went down to the shore. In their canoes they returned to their own land. It is from these seven who returned that we know of the abode of Manabush.

PEBOAN AND SEEGWAN

Ojibwa

Long ago an old man sat alone in his lodge beside a frozen stream. The fire was dying out, and it was near the end of winter. Outside the lodge, the cold wind swept before it the drifting snow. So the old man sat alone, day after day, until at last a young warrior entered his lodge. He was fresh and joyous and youthful.

The old man welcomed him. He drew out his long pipe and filled it with tobacco. He lighted it from the dying embers of the fire. Then they smoked together.

The old man said, "I blow my breath and the streams stand still. The water becomes stiff and hard like the stones."

"I breathe," said the warrior, "and flowers spring up over the plain."

"I shake my locks," said the old man, "and snow covers the land. Leaves fall from the trees. The birds fly away. The animals hide. The earth becomes hard."

"I shake my locks," said the young man, "and the warm rain falls. Plants blossom; the birds return; the streams flow."

Then the sun came up over the edge of the Earth-plain and began to climb the trail through the Sky-land. The old man slept. Behold! The frozen stream nearby began to flow. The fire in the lodge died out. Robins sat upon the lodge poles and sang.

Then the warrior looked upon the sleeping old man. Behold! It was Peboan, the Winter-maker.*

* In his lodge beside a river,
Close beside a frozen river,
Sat an old man, sad and lonely,
White his hair was as a snow-drift;
Dull and low his fire was burning,
And the old man shook and trembled,
. . . .
Hearing nothing but the tempest
As it roared along the forest,
Seeing nothing but the snow-storm,
As it whirled and hissed and drifted.
All the coals were white with ashes
And the fire was slowly dying,
As a young man, walking lightly,
At the open doorway entered.
Red with blood of youth his cheeks were,
Soft his eyes, as stars in Spring-time.

—*Hiawatha*

THE GRAVE FIRES

Ojibwa

A small war party of Ojibwas fought, long ago, with enemies on an open plain. Then their chief was shot by an arrow in his breast as he rode after the retreating enemy. When his warriors found their chief dead, they placed him, sitting, with his back against a tree. They left him there with his bow and arrows.

But the chief was not dead. He saw the warriors leave him and he ran after them as they rode the homeward trail. He followed closely in their trail. He slept in their camp, yet they did not see him.

When the war party reached their own village, they sang the song of victory, yet they sent up the death wail for those who were killed. The women and children came out. The chief heard his warriors tell of his death. He said, "No, I am not dead," but they did not hear him.

Then the chief went to his own wigwam. His wife was weeping, and wailing for his death. "I am here," he said, but she did not hear him. "I am hungry," he said. She made no answer. Only she raised again the death wail.

The chief thought. Perhaps only his spirit had returned. Perhaps his body was yet on the field of battle. So he followed the trail back to the battle field. It was a four days' journey. For three days he saw no one as he journeyed. The fourth day, on the edge of the plain, he saw a fire in his trail. He walked to one side and the other; the fire moved also and always burned before him. Then he turned in another direction. The fire was again in his trail. Then he sprang suddenly, and jumped through the flame.

At once he awoke. He was sitting on the ground, with his back against a tree. Over his head in the branches sat a large war eagle. Now Eagle was his guardian, because he had come to him in his fasting vision in his youth.

Then the wounded chief arose. He followed the trail of the war party to his village. Four days he followed the homeward trail. He came to a stream which flowed between him and his wigwam, therefore he gave the whoop which means the return of an absent friend. Then the Indians began to think. They said, "No one is absent. Perhaps it is an enemy." So they sent over a canoe with armed men. Thus the chief landed among his own people.

Then the chief gave them instructions. He said it was pleasing to a spirit to have a fire burning at the grave for four days after the body was buried. This was because it is four days' journey on the death trail to the Ghost-land; so the spirit needed a fire at his camping place every evening.

Also he said the spirit needed his bow and arrow, his best robes, in his journey. Therefore the Ojibwas burn a fire four nights at a new grave, that the spirit may be happy in following the Trail of the Dead to the Spirit-land.*

* Thus they buried Minnehaha.
And at night a fire was lighted,
On her grave four times was kindled,
For her soul upon its journey
To the Islands of the Blessed.
From his doorway Hiawatha
Saw it burning in the forest,
Lighting up the gloomy hemlocks;
From his sleepless bed uprising,
From the bed of Minnehaha,
Stood and watched it at the doorway,
That it might not be extinguished,
Might not leave her in the darkness.

—*Hiawatha*

THE DEATH TRAIL

Choctaw

After a man dies, he must travel far on the death trail. It journeys to the Darkening-land, where Sun slips over the edge of the Earth-plain. Then the spirit comes to a deep, rapid stream. There are steep and rugged hills on each side, so that one may not follow a land trail. The Trail of the Dead leads over the stream, and the only bridge is a pine log. It is a very slippery log, and even the bark has been peeled off. Also on the other side of the bridge are six persons. They have rocks in their hands, and throw them at spirits when they are just at the middle of the log.

Now when an evil spirit sees the stones coming, he tries to dodge them. Therefore he slips off the log. He falls far into the water below, where are evil things. The water carries him around and around, as in a whirlpool, and then brings him back again among the evil things. Sometimes evil spirit climbs up on the rocks and looks over into the country of the good spirits. But he cannot go there.

Now the good spirit walks over safely. He does not mind the stones and does not dodge them. He crosses the stream and goes to a good hunting land. It is more beautiful there than on the Earth-plain. There are no storms. The sky is always blue, and the grass is green, and there are many buffaloes. Therefore there is always feasting and dancing.

THE DUCK AND THE NORTH WEST WIND

Ojibwa

Once Shingebiss, the duck, lived all alone in his wigwam on the shore of a lake. It was winter and very cold. Ice had frozen over the top of the water. Shingebiss had but four logs of wood in his wigwam, but each log would burn one month and there were but four winter months.*

Shingebiss had no fear of the cold. He would go out on the coldest day. He would seek for places where rushes and flags grew through the ice. He pulled them up and dived through the broken ice for fish. Thus he had plenty of food. Thus he went to his wigwam dragging long strings of fish behind him on the ice.

* And at night Kabibonokka
To the lodge came, wild and wailing,
Heaped the snow in drifts about it,
Shouted down into the smoke-flue,
Shook the lodge poles in his fury,
Flapped the curtain of the doorway,
Shingebis, the diver, feared not,
Shingebis, the diver, cared not;
Four great logs had he for firewood,
One for each moon of the winter,
And for food the fishes served him,
By his blazing fire he sat there,
Warm and merry, eating, laughing,
Singing, "O Kabibonokka,
You are but my fellow mortal!"

—*Hiawatha*

North West noticed this. He said, "Shingebiss is a strange man. I will see if I cannot get the better of him."

North West shook his rattle and the wind blew colder. Snow drifted high. But Shingebiss did not let his fire go out. In the worst storms he continued going out, seeking for the weak places in the ice where the roots grew.

North West noticed this. He said, "Shingebiss is a strange man. I shall go and visit him."

That night North West went to the door of the wigwam. Shingebiss had cooked his fish and eaten it. He was lying on his side before the fire, singing songs.

He sang,

Ka neej Ka neej
Be in Be in
Bon in Bon in
Oc ee Oc ee
Ca We-ya Ca We-ya.

This meant, "Spirit of North West, you are but my fellow man."

Now he sang this because he knew North West was standing at the door of his wigwam. He could feel his cold breath. He kept right on singing his songs.

North West said, "Shingebiss is a strange man. I shall go inside."

Therefore North West entered the wigwam and sat down on the opposite side of the lodge. Shingebiss lay before the fire and sang: "Spirit of North West, you are but my fellow man."

Then he got up and poked the fire. The wigwam became very warm. At last North West said, "I cannot stand this. I must go out. Shingebiss is a very strange man." So he went out.

The North West shook his rattles until the great storms came. Thus there was much ice and snow and wind. All the flag roots were frozen in hard ice. Still Shingebiss went fishing. He bit off the frozen flags and rushes, and broke the hard ice around their roots. He dived for fish and went home dragging strings of fish behind him on the ice.

North West noticed this. He said, "Shingebiss must have very strong medicine. Some manito is helping him. I cannot conquer him. Shingebiss is a very strange man."

So he let him alone.

HOW THE HUNTER DESTROYED SNOW

Menomini

Once a hunter with his wife and two children lived in a tepee. Each day the hunter went out for game. He was a good hunter and he brought back much game.

But one day, after autumn had gone and winter had come, the hunter met Kon, Snow, who froze his feet badly. Then the hunter made a large wooden bowl and filled it with Kon. He buried it in a deep hole where the midday sun could shine down upon it, and where Snow could not run away. Then he covered the hole with sticks and leaves so that Snow would be a prisoner until summer.

Now when midsummer came, and everything was warm, the hunter came back to this hole and pulled away the sticks and leaves. He let the midday sun shine down upon Kon so that he melted. Thus the hunter punished Kon.

But when autumn came again, one day the hunter heard someone say to him, when he was in the forest: "You punished me last summer, but when winter comes I will show you how strong I am."

The hunter knew it was Kon's voice. He at once built another tepee, near the one in which he lived, and filled it full of firewood.

At last winter came again. When the hunter was in the forest one day, he heard Kon say, "Now I am coming to visit you, as I said I should. In four days I shall be at your tepee."

When the hunter returned home, he made ready more firewood; he built a fire at the two sides of the tepee. After four days, everything became frozen. It was very cold. The hunter kept up the fires in the tepee. He took out all the extra fur robes to cover his wife and children. The cold became more severe. It was hard not to freeze.

On the fifth day, towards night, the hunter looked out from his tepee upon a frozen world. Then he saw a stranger coming. He looked like any other stranger, except that he had a very large head and an immense beard. When he came to the tepee, the hunter asked him in. He at once came in, but he would not go near either of the fires. This puzzled the hunter and he began to watch the stranger.

It became colder and colder after the stranger had come into the tepee. The hunter added more wood to each of the fires until they roared. The stranger seemed too warm. The hunter added more wood, and the stranger became warmer and warmer. Then the hunter saw that as he became warm, he seemed to shrink. At last his head and body were quite small. Then the hunter knew who the stranger guest was. It was Kon, the Cold. So he kept up his fires until Kon melted altogether away.

THE PIPE OF PEACE

Ojibwa

In the olden days, so they say, the Indians fought much. Always they followed the war trail. Then Gitche Manito, the Good Mystery, thought, "This is not well. My children should not always follow the war trail." Therefore he called a great council. He called all the tribes together. Now this was on the upper Mississippi.

Gitche Manito stood on a great wall of red rock. On the green plain below him were the wigwams of his children. All the tribes were there.

Gitche Manito broke off a piece of the red rock. He made a pipe out of it. He made a pipe by turning it in his hands. Then he smoked the pipe, and the smoke made a great cloud in the sky.

He spoke in a loud voice. He said, "See, my people, this stone is red. It is red because it is the flesh of all tribes. Therefore can it be used only for a pipe of peace when you cease to follow the war trail. Therefore it is the Place of Peace. To all the tribes it belongs."

Then the cloud grew larger and Gitche Manito vanished in it.

Now therefore, because of the command of Gitche Manito, the Indians smoke the pipe of peace when they cease to follow the war trail. And because it is the Place of Peace, the tomahawk and the scalping knife are never lifted there.*

THE THUNDER'S NEST

Ojibwa

Thunder had a Nest where a very small bird sits upon her eggs during fair weather. When an egg hatches, the skies are rent with bolts of thunder.

* On the Mountains of the Prairie,
On the great Red Pipe-stone Quarry,
Gitche Manito, the mighty,
He the Master of Life descending,
On the red crags of the quarry,
Stood erect and called the nations,
Called the tribes of men together.
. . . .
"I am weary of your quarrels,
Weary of your wars and bloodshed,
Weary of your prayers for vengeance,
Of your wranglings and dissensions;
. . . .
Break the red stone from this quarry,
Mould and make it into Peace-pipes,
Take the reeds that grow beside you,
Deck them with your brightest feathers,
Smoke the calumet together."

—*Hiawatha*

THE PIPESTONE

Sioux

Before there were any people on the earth, Gitche Manito hunted the buffalo. He killed them and cooked them before his campfire on the Red Rocks, on the top of the Coteau des Prairies, the Mountain of the Prairies. So the blood of the buffaloes ran over the rocks and made them red.

Gitche Manito was then a very large bird. We can still see his tracks in the red stone. Now it happened a large snake crawled out of its hole to eat the eggs of the Bird. Then at once the egg hatched out in a clap of thunder.

Gitche Manito took a piece of stone to throw at the snake. He shaped it in his hands like to a man.

Now this man's feet stood fast in the ground where he was. Thus he stayed for many ages; therefore he grew very old. He was older than a hundred men at the present time. At last another tree grew beside him. It grew a long while, until a snake bit off the roots. Then the two people left the pipestone quarry. They wandered away. They were the grandfathers of all the tribes.

THE PIPESTONE

Knisteneaux

A great flood came. Then the tribes met on the Coteau des Prairies, on the Mountain of the Prairies, to get out of the way of the waters. Then the waters rose higher; thus the tribes were drowned. Gitche Manito made them into stone. Therefore the stone is red.

Now when the waters were rising, a young woman caught the foot of a large bird flying near. It was War-eagle. He carried her to the top of a large mountain. Thus she was saved. Then she married War-eagle.

Now all the tribes were drowned. Therefore the children of War-eagle and the Indian woman were the ancestors of all the Indians.

PAU-PUK-KEE-WIS

Ojibwa

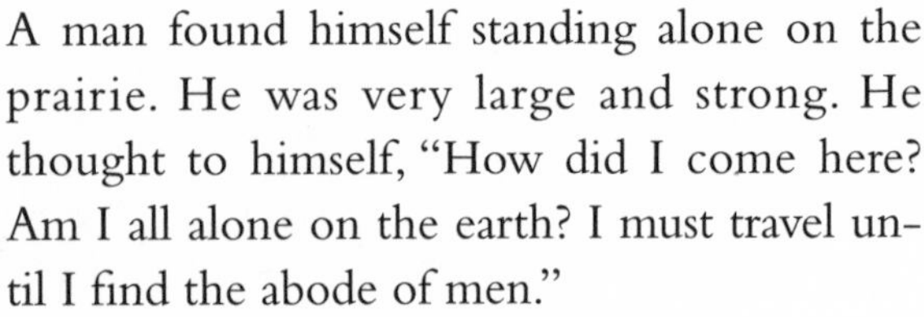

A man found himself standing alone on the prairie. He was very large and strong. He thought to himself, "How did I come here? Am I all alone on the earth? I must travel until I find the abode of men."

So he started out. After a long time he came to a wood. There were decayed stumps there, very old, as if cut in the olden times. Again he journeyed a long time. He came to a wood in which there were more stumps, newly cut. Then he came to the fresh trail of people. He saw wood just cut, lying in heaps. At sunset he came out of the forest. He saw a village of many lodges standing on rising ground.

He said, "I will go there on the run." He ran. When he came to the first lodge, he sprang over it. Those within saw something pass over the smoke hole. They heard a thump on the ground.

They said, "What is that?" They ran out. They invited him to enter. Many warriors were in the wigwam, and an old chief.

The chief said, "Where are you going? What is your name?"

He said, "I am in search of adventures. I am Pau-puk-kee-wis." Then they laughed.

After a short time he went on. A young man went with him as his *mesh-in-au-wa,* as his pipe bearer.

As they journeyed, Pau-puk-kee-wis did strange things. He leaped over trees. He whirled on one foot until dust clouds were flying.

One day a large village of wigwams came in their trail. They went to it. The chief told them of evil manitoes who had killed all the people going to that village. War parties had been sent against them. The warriors were all killed.

Pau-puk-kee-wis said, "I will go and visit them."

The chief said, "Oh no. They are evil. They will kill you."

Pau-puk-kee-wis said, "I will go and visit them."

Then the chief said, "I will send twenty warriors with you."

So Pau-puk-kee-wis, with his pipe bearer and twenty warriors, started off at once. They came near that lodge. Pau-puk-kee-wis said, "Hide here. Thus you will be safe. You will see what I do." He went to that lodge. He entered.

The manitoes were very ugly. They were evil looking. There were a father and four sons. They offered him food. He refused it.

The old manito said, "What have you come for?"

"Nothing," said Pau-puk-kee-wis.

"Do you want to wrestle?" asked the manito.

"Yes," said Pau-puk-kee-wis.

At once the eldest brother rose and they began to wrestle. These manitoes were very evil. They wished to kill Pau-puk-kee-wis in order to eat him. But that man was very strong. He tripped the manito. Then he threw him down. His head struck on a stone.

The next brother wrestled with Pau-puk-kee-wis. He fell. Then the other two wrestled. All four fell on the ground. The old manito began to run. Pau-puk-kee-wis pursued him. He pursued him in a very queer way, just for fun. Sometimes he leaped over him and ran ahead. Sometimes he pushed him ahead from behind.

All the twenty warriors cried, "Ha! ha! ha! Ha! ha! ha! Pau-puk-kee-wis is driving him."

At last Pau-puk-kee-wis killed him. Thus all the evil manitoes were dead.

Then they looked on the bones of the warriors and people who had been killed by those evil ones. Then Pau-puk-kee-wis took three arrows. He performed a ceremony to Gitche Manito. He shot one arrow. He cried, "You who are lying down, rise up or you will be hit." At once the bones all moved to one place.

He shot a second arrow. He cried, "You who are lying down, rise up, or you will be hit." The proper bones moved together, toward each other.

He shot a third arrow. He cried, "You who are lying down, rise up, or you will be hit." The people became alive again. Then Pau-puk-kee-wis led them back to the village of the friendly chief.

This one then came to him with his council. He said, "You should rule my people. You only are able to defend them."

Pau-puk-kee-wis said, "I am going on a journey. Let my pipe bearer be chief." So he was.

Pau-puk-kee-wis began his journey. "Ho! ho! ho!" cried all the people. "Come back again. Ho! ho! ho!"

He journeyed on. He came to a lake made by beavers.*

* With a smile he spake in this wise:
"O, my friend, Ahmeek, the beaver,
Cool and pleasant is the water;
Let me dive into the water,
Let me rest there in your lodges;
Change me, too, into a beaver!"
Cautiously replied the beaver,
With reserve he thus made answer,
"Let me first consult the others,
Let me ask the other beavers."

—*Hiawatha*

He stood on the beaver dam and watched. He saw the head of a beaver peering out.

"Make me a beaver like yourself," said Pau-puk-kee-wis. He wanted to see how beavers lived.

"I will go and ask what the others have to say," said Beaver.

Soon all the beavers looked out to see if he were armed. He had left his bow and arrow in a hollow tree.

"Make me a beaver," said Pau-puk-kee-wis. "I wish to live among you."

"Yes," said Beaver chief. "Lie down." He lay down. He found himself a beaver.

"You must make me large," he said.

"Yes," said Beaver chief. "When we get into the lodge, you shall be made very large."

So they all dived down into the water again. They passed heaps of tree limbs and logs lying on the bottom of the river.

"What are these for?" asked Pau-puk-kee-wis.

"For our winter food," said Beaver chief.

Now when they got into the lodge, they made Pau-puk-kee-wis very large. They made him ten times larger than themselves.

Soon a beaver came running in. He cried, "The Indians are hunting us." At once all the beavers ran out of the lodge door on the bottom of the river. Pau-puk-kee-wis was too large. He could not get out. The Indians broke down the dam. They lowered the water. They broke in the lodge. They saw that one.

"Ty-au! Ty-au!" cried the Indians. *"Me-sham-mek,* the chief of the beavers, is here."

So they killed him. Yet Pau-puk-kee-wis kept thinking. They placed his great body on a pole. Seven or eight Indians carried it. They went back to their lodges. They sent out invitations for a great feast. Then the women came out to skin him on the snow. When his flesh became cold, the *Jee-bi* of Pau-puk-kee-wis went away. His spirit went away.

So Pau-puk-kee-wis found himself standing alone on a prairie. Soon there came nearby a heard of elk. He thought, "They are very happy. I will be an elk." He went near them, and said, "Make me an elk. I wish to live among you."

They said, "Yes. Get down on your hands and knees."

Soon he found himself an elk.

"I want big horns and big feet," said Pau-puk-kee-wis. "I want to be very large."

"Yes, yes," said the elk. So they made him very large. At last they said, "Are you large enough?" Pau-puk-kee-wis said, "Yes."

So he lived with the elks. One cold day they all went into the woods for shelter. Soon some of the herd came racing by like a strong wind. At once all began to run.

"Keep out on the prairies," they said to Pau-puk-kee-wis.

But he was so large he got tangled up in the thick woods. He soon smelt the hunters. They were all following his trail. Pau-puk-kee-wis jumped high. He broke down saplings. Then the hunters shot him. He jumped higher. He jumped over the tree tops. Then all the hunters shot him, so they killed him. Then they skinned him. When his flesh became cold, the spirit of Pau-puk-kee-wis went away.

Thus Pau-puk-kee-wis had many adventures. After a long time Manabozho killed him. Then he was really dead because he was killed in his human form. Manabozho said, "You shall not be permitted to live on the earth again. I will make you a war eagle."

Thus Pau-puk-kee-wis became a war eagle. He lives in the sky.

IAGOO, THE BOASTER*

Ojibwa

Iagoo was a great boaster. Once he told the people of a water lily he had seen. He said the leaf was large enough to make garments for his wife and daughter.

One evening Iagoo was sitting in his wigwam, on the bank of the river. He heard ducks quack on the stream. He shot at them, without aiming. He shot through the door of the wigwam. Behold! His arrow pierced a swan flying by. It killed many ducks in the stream. The arrow flew farther. It killed two loons, just coming up from beneath the water. Then it killed a very large fish.

Iagoo went hunting. He followed the trail of the deer through the forest. He shot a deer and skinned it. He lifted the meat upon his shoulders. As he came from his hunting place, Iagoo saw a person on a prairie before him. He pursued that person. Iagoo ran half a day after that one. Then he remembered the meat upon his shoulders. He remembered he carried the body of the deer.

* From his lodge went Pau-puk-keewis,
Came with speed into the village,
Found the young men all assembled
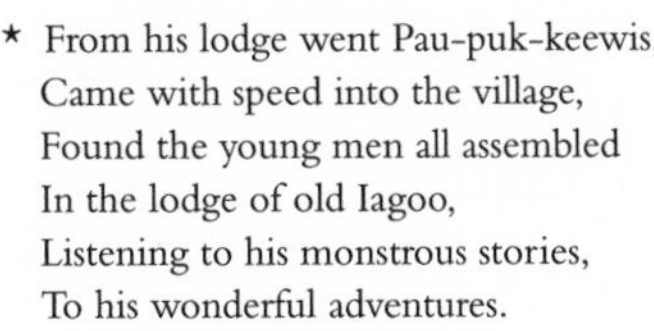
In the lodge of old Iagoo,
Listening to his monstrous stories,
To his wonderful adventures.

. . . .

Homeward now returned Iagoo,
The great traveller, the great boaster,
Full of new and strange adventures,
Marvels many and many wonders.

—*Hiawatha*

Iagoo had many adventures. He found mosquitoes in a bog-land. They were very large. The wing of one he used for a sail for his canoe, when the breeze blew. The nose of that insect was as large as his wife's digging stick.

One day Iagoo watched a beaver's lodge. He watched for the peering head of a beaver. Behold! An ant went by. She had killed a hare. She dragged hare's body on the ground behind her.

OJEEG, THE SUMMER-MAKER

Ojibwa

Ojeeg was a great hunter. He lived on the southern shore of Lake Superior. Ojeeg had a wife and one son.

Now the son hunted game as the father taught him. He followed the trails over the snow. For snow lay always on the ground. It was always cold. Therefore the boy returned home crying.

One day as he went to his father's wigwam in the cold and snow he saw Red Squirrel, gnawing the end of a pine cone. Now the son of Ojeeg had shot nothing all day because his hands were so cold. When he saw Red Squirrel, he came nearer, and raised his bow.

Red Squirrel said, "My grandson, put up your arrow. Listen to me."

The boy put the arrow in his quiver.

Red Squirrel said, "You pass my wigwam

very often. You cry because you cannot kill birds. Your fingers are numb with cold. Obey me. Thus it shall always be summer. Thus you can kill many birds."

Red Squirrel said again, "Obey me. When you reach your father's wigwam, throw down your bow and arrows. Begin to weep. If your mother says, 'My son, what is the matter?' do not answer her. Continue weeping. If she says, 'My son, eat this,' you must refuse the food. Continue weeping. In the evening when your father comes in he will say to your mother, 'What is the matter with my son?' She will say, 'He came in crying. He will not tell me.' Your father will say, 'My son, what is the matter? I am a spirit. Nothing is too hard for me.' Then you must answer, 'It is always cold and dreary. Snow lies always upon the ground. Melt the snow, my father, so that we may have always summer.' Then your father will say, 'It is very difficult to do what you ask. I will try.' Then you must be quiet. You must eat the food they give you."

Thus it happened.

Ojeeg then said, "I must make a feast. I must invite my friends to go on this journey with me." At once Ojeeg killed a bear. The next day he had a great feast. There were Otter, Beaver, and Lynx. Also Wolverine and Badger were at the feast.

Then they started on their journey. On the twentieth day they came to the foot of a high mountain. There was blood in the trail. Some person had killed an animal. They followed the trail of that person. They arrived at a wigwam.

Ojeeg said, "Do not laugh. Be very quiet."

A man stood in the doorway of the wigwam. He was a great manito. He was a head only. Thus he was very strange. Then he made a feast for them. He made very curious movements, so Otter laughed. At once the manito leaped upon him. He sprang on him, but Otter slipped out from under him and escaped.

The manito and the animals talked all night. The manito said to Ojeeg, the Fisher, "You will succeed. You will be the summer-maker. But you will die. Yet the summer will come."

Now when they followed the trail in the morning, they met Otter. He was very cold and hungry, therefore Fisher gave him meat.

Then they journeyed on. On the twentieth day, they came to the top of a lofty mountain. Then they smoked their pipes.

Then Ojeeg, the Fisher, and the animals prepared themselves. Ojeeg said to Otter, "We must first make a hole in the Sky-cover. You try first."

Otter made a great spring. He did not even touch the Sky-cover. He fell back, down the hill, to the bottom of the hill. Then Otter said, "I will go home." So he did.

Then Beaver tried. He fell. Also Lynx and Badger fell.

Then Wolverine tried. He made a great leap and touched the sky. Then he leaped again. He pressed against the Sky-cover. He leaped a third time. The Sky-cover broke, and Wolverine went into the Sky-land. Fisher also sprang in quickly after him.

Thus Wolverine and Fisher were in the Sky-plain, in the summer land. There were many flowers and streams of bright water. There were birds in the trees, and fish and water birds on the streams. Many lodges stood there, but they were empty. In each lodge were many *mocuks,* many bird cages, with birds in them.

At once Ojeeg began to cut the *mocuks.* The birds flew out. They flew down through the hole in the Sky-cover to the Earth-plain below. They carried warm air down with them.

Now when the people of the Sky-land saw these strangers, and their birds escaping, they ran to their wigwams. But they were too late. Spring, and summer, and autumn had slipped down the hole in the Sky-cover. Endless summer was just passing through, but they broke it in two with a blow. Therefore only a part of endless summer came down to the Earth-plain.

Now when Wolverine heard the noise of the sky people, running to their lodges, he jumped down the hole and escaped. Fisher also tried to jump, but the people had shut the cover. Therefore Fisher ran and the people pursued him. He climbed a great tree in the north, and the people began shooting at him. Now Fisher was a spirit; he could not be hurt except in the tip of his tail. At last they shot him in his tail.

Fisher called to the Sky People to stop shooting. But they did not stop until darkness came. Then they went away. Fisher climbed down. He went towards the north. He said, "I have kept my promise to my son. The seasons will now be different. There will be many moons without snow and cold."

Thus Fisher died, with the arrow sticking in his tail. It can be seen there, even to this day.*

* He was telling them the story
Of Ojeeg the Summer-Maker,
How he made a hole in heaven,
How he climbed up into heaven,
And let out the summer-weather,
The perpetual summer-weather.
How the Otter first essayed it,
How the Beaver, Lynx, and Badger,
Tried in turn the great achievement,
From the summit of the mountain . . .

—*Hiawatha*

PART THREE

Rabbit · Lynx · Owl

RABBIT GOES DUCK HUNTING

Cherokee

Rabbit was very boastful. One day he met Otter. Otter said, "Sometimes I eat ducks."

"Well, I eat ducks, too," said Rabbit.

So they went up the stream until they saw several ducks in the water. They followed the trail softly. Then they stood on the river bank.

Rabbit said, "You go first." At once Otter dived from the bank. He swam underwater until he reached a duck; then he pulled it under quickly so that the other ducks were not frightened. While he was underwater, Rabbit peeled bark from a sapling and made a noose.

"Now, watch me," he said, when Otter came back. He dived in and swam under water until he was nearly choked. So he came to the top to breathe. He did this several times. The last time he came up among the ducks and threw the noose over the head of one.

Duck spread her wings and flew up, with Rabbit hanging to the end of the noose. Up and up flew the duck, but Rabbit could not hold on any longer. Then he let go and dropped.

Rabbit fell into a hollow sycamore. It was very tall, and had no hole at the bottom. Rabbit stayed there until he was so hungry he ate his own fur, even as he does to this day.

After many days, he heard children playing around the tree. He began to sing,

Cut a door and look at me,
I'm the prettiest thing you ever did see.

The children at once ran home to tell their father. He came and cut a hole in the tree. As he chopped away, Rabbit kept singing,

Cut it larger, so you can see me. I am very pretty.

So they made the hole larger. Then Rabbit told them to stand back so they could get a good look at him. They stood back. Then Rabbit sprang out and leaped away.

RABBIT AND THE TAR BABY

Biloxi

Rabbit aided his friend the Frenchman with his work. They planted potatoes. Rabbit looked upon the potato vines as his share of the crop and ate them all.

Again Rabbit aided his friend the Frenchman. This time they planted corn. When it was grown, Rabbit said, "This time I will eat the roots." So he pulled up all the corn by the roots, but he found nothing to satisfy his hunger.

Then the Frenchman said, "Let us dig a well." Rabbit said, "No. You dig it alone."

The Frenchman said, "Then you shall not drink water from the well."

"That does not matter," said Rabbit. "I am

used to licking off the dew from the ground."

So the Frenchman dug his well. Then he made a tar baby and stuck it up close to the well. One day Rabbit came near the well, carrying a long piece of hollow cane and a tin bucket. When he reached the well he spoke to the tar baby; it did not answer.

"Friend, what is the matter? Are you angry?" asked Rabbit.

Tar baby did not answer. So Rabbit hit him with a forepaw. The forepaw stuck there.

"Let me go," said Rabbit, "or I will hit you on the other side."

Tar baby paid no attention, so Rabbit hit him with the other forepaw, and that stuck fast.

"I will kick you," said Rabbit. But when he kicked him the hindpaw stuck.

"Very well," he said, "I will kick you with the other foot." So he kicked him with the other foot and that stuck fast. By that time Rabbit looked like a ball, all four paws sticking to the tar baby.

Just then the Frenchman came to the well. He picked Rabbit up, tied his paws together, laid him down, and scolded him. Rabbit pretended to be in great fear of a brier patch.

"If you are so afraid of a brier patch," said the Frenchman, "I will throw you into one."

"Oh, no, no!" said Rabbit.

"I will throw you into the brier patch," repeated the Frenchman.

"I am much afraid of it," answered Rabbit.

"Since you are in such dread of it, I will throw you into it," said the Frenchman. So he picked up Rabbit and threw him far into the brier patch. Rabbit fell far away from the Frenchman.

Then he picked himself up and ran off, laughing at the trick he had played on the Frenchman.

RABBIT AND TAR WOLF

Cherokee

Once the weather was dry for so long that there was no more water in the springs and creeks. The animals held a council to see what to do about it. They decided to dig a well, and all agreed to help, except Rabbit who was a lazy fellow.

Rabbit said, "I don't need to dig for water. The dew on the grass is enough for me."

The others did not like this, but they all started to dig the well. It stayed dry for a long while and even the water in the well was low. Still Rabbit was lively and bright.

"Rabbit steals our water at night," they said. So they made a wolf of pine gum and tar. They set it by the well to scare the thief.

That night Rabbit came again to the well. He saw the black thing there.

"Who's there?" he asked. But Tar Wolf did not answer. Rabbit came nearer. Yet Tar Wolf did not move. Rabbit grew brave and said, "Get out of my way."

Tar Wolf did not move. So Rabbit hit him with his paw; but it stuck fast in the gum.

Rabbit became angry and said, "Let go my paw!" Still Tar Wolf said nothing. So Rabbit hit him with his hind foot; that stuck in the gum.

So Tar Wolf held Rabbit fast until morning. Then the other animals came for water. When they found Rabbit stuck fast, they made great fun of him for a while. At last Rabbit managed to get away.

RABBIT AND PANTHER

Menomini

Rabbit was great boaster. He wanted a medicine lodge and to have people think he was a great medicine man.

Now one day, Wabus, the Rabbit, and his wife were traveling. They came to a low hill covered with poplar sprouts. They were green and tender. Therefore Rabbit decided to make his home there.

Rabbit went first to the top of a hill and built a wigwam. He made trails from it in all directions, so he might see anyone who approached.

When the wigwam was finished, Rabbit told his wife he was going to dance; but first he ran all about the hill to see if anyone was watching him. He found no trail. Then he returned and began his song.

Now just as Rabbit returned to his wigwam, Panther reached the base of the hill, and he found Rabbit's trail. He followed it until he reached the place where Rabbit and his wife were dancing. Here he hid to watch Rabbit.

Now Rabbit told his wife to sit at one end of the lodge while he went to the other. He took his medicine bag. Then he approached her four times, chanting,

Ye ha-a-a-a-a Ye ha-a-a-a-a
Ye ha-a-a-a-a Ye ha-a-a-a-a

Then he shot at his wife, just as a medicine man does when he shoots at a new member. Then Rabbit's wife arose and shot at him. Thus they were very happy.

Then Rabbit began to sing a song which meant this: "If Panther comes across my trail while I am biting the bark from the poplars, he will not be able to catch me for I am a good runner."

When he had finished his song, Rabbit told his wife he would go out hunting. Panther waited for his return.

Now as Rabbit started home again he was very happy. But when he reached Panther's hiding place, his enemy sprang on his trail. Rabbit saw him and started back on his trail. Panther raced after him. He caught him and said, "You are the man who said I could not catch you. Now who is the fastest runner?" And before Rabbit could answer Panther ate him up. But Rabbit was such a boastful man.

HOW RABBIT STOLE OTTER'S COAT

Cherokee

All the animals were of different sizes and wore different coats. Some wore long fur and others wore short fur. Some had rings on their tails; others had no tails at all. The coats of the animals were of many colors—brown, or black, or yellow, or gray.

The animals were always quarreling about whose coat was the finest. Therefore they held a council to decide the matter.

Now everyone had heard a great deal about

Otter, but he lived far up the trail; he did not often visit the others. It was said he had the finest coat of all, but it was so long since they had seen him that no one remembered what it was like. They did not even know just where he lived, but they knew he would come when he heard of the council.

Rabbit was afraid the council would say that Otter had the finest coat. He learned by what trail Otter would come to the council. Then he went a four days' march up the trail to meet him. At last he saw Otter coming. He knew him at once by his beautiful coat of soft brown fur.

Otter said, "Where are you going?"

"They sent me to bring you to the council," answered Rabbit. "They were afraid you might not know the trail."

So Rabbit turned back and they traveled together. They traveled all day. At night Rabbit picked out a camping place. Otter was a stranger in that part. Rabbit cut down bushes for beds and made everything comfortable. Next morning they started on again.

In the afternoon, Rabbit picked up pieces of bark and wood, as they followed the trail, and loaded them on his back.

"Why are you doing that?" asked Otter.

"So that we may be warm and comfortable tonight," said Rabbit. Near sunset they stopped and made camp. After supper Rabbit began to whittle a stick, shaving it down to a paddle.

"Why are you doing that?" asked Otter again.

"Oh," said Rabbit, "I have good dreams when I sleep with a paddle under my head."

When the paddle was finished, Rabbit began to cut a good trail through the bushes to the river.

"Why are you doing that?" asked Otter.

"This is called 'The Place Where It Rains Fire,' and sometimes it does rain fire here," said Rabbit. "The sky looks a little that way tonight. You go to sleep and I will sit up and watch. If you hear me shout, you run and jump into the river. Better hang your coat on that limb over there, so it will not get burned."

Otter did as Rabbit told him; then both curled up and Otter went to sleep. But Rabbit stayed awake. After a while the fire burned down to red coals. Rabbit called to Otter; he was fast asleep. Then he called again, but Otter did not awaken.

Then Rabbit rose softly. He filled the paddle with hot coals, threw them up into the air and shouted, "It's raining fire! It's raining fire!"

The hot coals fell on Otter and he jumped up.

"To the river," shouted Rabbit, and Otter fled into the water. So he has lived in the water ever since.

Rabbit at once took Otter's coat and put it on, leaving his own behind. Then he followed the trail to the council.

All the animals were waiting for Otter. At last they saw him coming down the trail. They said to each other, "Otter is coming!" They sent one of the small animals to show him the best seat. After he was seated, the animals all went up in turn to welcome him. But Otter kept his head down with one paw over his face.

The animals were surprised. They did not know Otter was so bashful. At last Bear pulled the paw away. There was Rabbit! He sprang up and started to run. Bear struck at him and pulled the tail off his coat. But Rabbit was too quick and got safely away.

RABBIT AND BEAR

Biloxi

Rabbit and Bear had been friends for some time. One day Rabbit said to Bear, "Come and visit me. I live in a very large brier patch." Then he went home.

When he reached home he went out and gathered a quantity of young canes which he hung up.

After a while Bear reached a place near his house, but was seeking the large brier patch. Now Rabbit really dwelt in a very small patch. When Rabbit found that Bear was near, he began to make a pattering sound with his feet.

Bear was scared. He retreated to a distance and then stopped and stood listening. As soon as Rabbit saw this, he cried out, "Halloo! my friend! Was it you whom I treated in that manner? Come and take a seat."

So Bear went back to Rabbit's house and took a seat. Rabbit gave the young canes to his guest, who swallowed them all. Rabbit nibbled now and then at one, while Bear swallowed all the others.

"This is what I have always liked," said Bear when he went home. "Come and visit me. I dwell in a large bent tree."

Not long after, Rabbit started on his journey. He spent some time seeking the large bent tree but he could not find it. Bear lived in a hollow tree, and he sat there growling. Rabbit heard the growls and fled for some distance before he sat down.

Then Bear called, "Halloo! my friend! Was it you whom I treated in that manner? Come here and sit down."

Rabbit did so.

Bear said, "You are now my guest, but there is nothing for you to eat." So Bear went in search of food.

Bear went to gather young canes, but as he went along, he gathered also the small black bugs which live in decayed logs. When he had been gone some time, he returned to his lodge with only a few young canes. He put them down before Rabbit and then walked around him in a circle. In a little while, he offered Rabbit the black bugs.

"I have never eaten such food," said Rabbit.

Bear was offended. He said, "When I was your guest, I ate all the food you gave me, as I liked it very well. Now when I offer you food, why do you treat me in this way?" Then Bear said, also, "Before the sun sets, I shall kill you."

Rabbit's heart beat hard from terror, for Bear stood at the entrance of the hollow log to prevent his escape. But Rabbit was very nimble. He dodged first this way and then that, and with a long leap he got out of the hollow tree. He went at once to his brier patch and sat down.

Rabbit was very angry with Bear. He shouted to him, "When people are hunting you, I will go toward your hiding place, and show them where you are."

That is why, when dogs hunt a rabbit, they always shoot a bear. That is all.

WHY DEER NEVER EAT MEN

Menomini

After Rabbit had decided about light and darkness, he saw Owasse, the Bear, coming.

Rabbit said, "Bear, what do you want for food?" Bear said, "Acorns and fruit."

Then Rabbit asked Fish Hawk. He said, "Fish Hawk, what will you select for your food?"

Fish Hawk said, "I will take that fellow, Sucker, lying in the water there."

Sucker said at once, "You may eat me if you can, but that has still to be decided."

Sucker at once swam out into the deepest part of the river, where Fish Hawk could not reach him. Then Fish Hawk rose into the air to a point where his shadow fell exactly on the spot where Sucker lay. Now as Sucker lay there, he saw the shadow of a large bird on the bed of the stream. He became frightened. He thought, "It must be a manito," so he swam slowly to the surface. At once Fish Hawk darted down on him and carried him into the air. Then he ate him.

Rabbit looked about him again. He saw Moqwaio, the Wolf. He cried, "Ho, Wolf! What do you wish for food?"

Wolf said, "I will eat Deer." Deer said, "You cannot eat me, because I can run too swiftly." Wolf said, "We will see about that." So they had a race. Deer started ahead and ran very swiftly. Wolf ran swiftly, too, but his fur robe was too heavy. At last he thought, "This robe is too heavy. I will slip it off." So he threw it off. Then he bounded ahead and caught Deer and ate him.

Then Rabbit asked another Deer, of the same totem, "Deer, what will you select as food?"

Deer said, "I will eat people. There are many Indians in the country. I will eat them."

At once all the animals began to talk. They said to Deer, "The Indian is too powerful. You can never eat him."

Deer said, "Well, I will plan to eat Indians, anyway." Then he walked off.

Now one day an Indian was out hunting. He saw deer tracks to the right and so followed them. They went in a large circle until they brought him back where he had started. Then he saw deer tracks to the left. So he followed those, until they also brought him back, in a large circle, to the point where he started. Then the Indian saw that Deer was following him.

Deer was determined to eat the Indians, because there were many of them. It would not be difficult to hunt for food. But first he wanted to frighten the hunter. So he pulled two ribs from his sides, and stuck them into his lower jaw. They looked like tusks. Deer looked very fierce. Then Deer came walking along, looking for an Indian. But the hunter raised his bow and shot Deer. He carried the deer meat back to his wigwam.

The shade of Deer at once went to the council of birds and animals. He told Rabbit all about it.

Rabbit said, "I told you that you could not eat people. You see how it is? Now you will have to live on grass and twigs."

And so they do, even to this day.

HOW RABBIT SNARED THE SUN

Biloxi

Rabbit and his grandmother lived in a wigwam. Rabbit used to go hunting every day, very early in the morning. But no matter how early he went, a person leaving long footprints had passed along ahead of him. Each morning Rabbit thought, "I will reach there before him." Yet each morning the person leaving long footprints passed before him.

One morning Rabbit said to his grandmother, "Oh, Grandmother, although I have long wished to be the first to get there, again has he got there ahead of me. Oh, Grandmother, I will make a noose, and I will place it in the trail of that one, and thus I will catch him."

"Why should you do that?" asked Grandmother.

"I hate that person," said Rabbit. He departed. When he reached there, he found that the person had already departed. So he lay down near by and waited for night. Then he went to the trail where the person with long feet had been passing, and set a snare.

Very early the next morning he went to look at his trap. Behold! Sun had been caught. Rabbit ran home very quickly.

"Oh, Grandmother, I have caught something but it scares me. I wished to take the noose, but it scared me every time I went to get it."

Then Rabbit took a knife and again went

there. The person said, "You have done very wrong. Come and release me."

Rabbit did not go directly toward him. He went to one side. He bent his head low and cut the cord. At once Sun went above on his trail. But Rabbit had been so near him that Sun burned his fur on the back of his neck.

Rabbit ran home. He cried, "Oh, Grandmother, I have been severely burned."

"Alas! My grandson has been severely burned," said Grandmother.

WHEN THE ORPHAN TRAPPED THE SUN

Ojibwa

Animals and men lived on the earth in the beginning. The animals killed all the people except a girl and her tiny brother, who hid from them. The brother did not grow at all. Therefore when the sister collected firewood, she took him with her. She made him a bow and arrow.

One day she said, "Now I must leave you for a while. Soon the snowbirds will come and pick worms out of the wood I have cut. Shoot one of them and bring it to me."

The boy waited. The birds came and he shot at them with his arrows. He could not kill one. The next day he shot at them again.

Then he killed one. He came back to the wigwam with a bird.

He said, "My sister, skin it. I will wear the skins of the snowbirds."

"What shall we do with the body?" she asked.

"Cut it in two. We will put it in our broth." Now at that time, the animals were very large. People did not eat them.

The boy killed ten snowbirds. Then his sister made a coat for him. One day he said, "Are we alone on the Earth-plain?'

She said, "The animals who live in such a place have killed all our relatives. You must never go there." Therefore he went in that direction.

Now he walked a long while and met no one. Then he lay down on a knoll where the sun had melted the snow. He fell asleep. Then Sun looked down at him and burned his bird-skin coat. He tightened it so that the boy was bound into it. When he awoke, the boy said to Sun, "You are not too high. I will pay you back."

He went home. He said to his sister, "Sun has spoiled my coat." He would not eat. He lay down on the ground. He lay ten days on one side. Then he turned over and lay ten days on the other side.

At last he rose. He said to his sister, "Make me a snare. I shall catch Sun."

She said, "I have no string." The boy said, "Make a string." Then she remembered a bit of dried sinew which her father had had. So she made a snare for him.

The boy said, "That will not do. Make a better snare." She said, "I have no string." At last she remembered. She cut off some of her hair. She made a string from that.

The boy said, "That will not do. Make me a noose." She thought again. Then she remembered. She went out of the wigwam. She took something. She made a braid out of that thing.

The boy said, "This will do." He was much pleased. When he took it, it became a long red cord. There was much of it. He wound it around his body.

The boy left the wigwam while Sun was at home. He did this so that he might catch him as he came over the edge of the earth. He put the noose at the spot just where Sun came over the edge. When Sun came along, the noose caught his head. He was held tight, so that he could not follow his trail in the Sky-land.

Now the animals who ruled the earth were frightened because Sun did not follow the trail. They said, "What shall we do?" So they called a great council. They said, "We must send someone to cut the noose." Thus they spoke in the council.

Now all the animals were afraid to cut the cord. Sun was so hot he would burn them. At last Dormouse said, "I will go." He stood up in the council. He was as high as a mountain. He was the largest of all the animals.

When Dormouse reached the place where Sun was snared, his fur began to singe and his back to burn. It was very hot. Dormouse cut the cord with his teeth. But so much of him was burned up, he became very small. Therefore Dormouse is the smallest of animals. That is why he is called Kug-e-been-gwa-kwa.

THE HARE AND THE LYNX

Ojibwa

Once there was a little white hare, living in a wigwam with her grandmother. Now Grandmother sent Hare back to her native land. When Hare had gone a short way, Lynx came down the trail. Lynx sang:

Where, pretty white one,
Where, pretty white one,
Where do you go?

"Tshwee! Tshwee! Tshwee! Tshwee!" cried Hare, and ran back to Grandmother.

"See, Grandmother," she said, "Lynx came down the trail and sang,

Where, pretty white one,
Where, pretty white one,
Where do you go?"

"Ho!" said Grandmother. "Have courage! Tell Lynx you are going to your native land."

Hare went back up the trail. Lynx stood there, so Hare sang,

To the point of land I go,
There is the home of the little white one,
There I go.

Lynx looked at the trembling little hare, and began to sing again,

Little white one, tell me,
Little white one, tell me,
Why are your ears so thin and dry?

"Tshwee! Tshwee! Tshwee! Tshwee!" cried little Hare, and ran back to Grandmother.

"See, Grandmother," said Hare, "Lynx came down the trail and sang,

Little white one, tell me,
Little white one, tell me,
Why are your ears so thin and dry?

"Ho!" said Grandmother, "Go and tell him your uncles made them so when they came from the South."

So Hare ran up the trail and sang,

My uncles came from the south;
They made my ears as they are.
They made them thin and dry.

And then Hare laid her little pink ears back upon her shoulders, and started to go to the point of land. But Lynx sang again,

Why do you go away, little white one?
Why do you go away, little white one?
Why are your feet so dry and swift?

"Tshwee! Tshwee! Tshwee! Tshwee!" cried Hare and again she ran back to Grandmother.

"Ho! Do not mind him," said Grandmother. "Do not listen to him. Do not answer him. Just run straight on."

So the little white hare ran up the trail as fast as she could. When she came to the place where Lynx had stood, he was gone. So Hare ran on and had almost reached her native land, on the point of land, when Lynx sprang out of the thicket and ate her up.

WELCOME TO A BABY

Cherokee

Little Wren is the messenger of the Birds. She pries into everything. She gets up early in the morning and goes around to every wigwam to get news for the Bird council. When a new baby comes into a wigwam, she finds out whether it is a boy or a girl.

If it is a boy, the Bird council sings mournfully, "Alas! The whistle of the arrow! My shins will burn!" Because the Birds all know that when the boy grows older he will hunt them with his bows and arrows, and will roast them on a stick.

But if the baby is a girl, they are glad. They sing, "Thanks! The sound of the pestle! In her wigwam I shall surely be able to scratch where she sweeps." Because they know that when she grows older and beats the corn into meal, they will be able to pick up stray grains.

Cricket also is glad when the baby is a girl. He sings, "Thanks! I shall sing in the wigwam where she lives." But if it is a boy, Cricket laments, "*Gwo-he!* He will shoot me! He will shoot me! He will shoot me!" Because boys make little bows to shoot crickets and grasshoppers.

When the Cherokee Indians hear of a new baby, they ask, "Is it a bow, or a meal sifter?" Or else they ask, "Is it ball-sticks or bread?"

BABY SONG

Cherokee

Ha wi ye hy u we,
Ha wi ye hy u we.
Yu we yu we he,
Ha wi ye hy u we.

The Bear is very bad, so they say.
Long time ago he was very bad, so they say.
The Bear did so and so, they say.

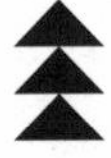

SONG TO THE FIREFLY

Ojibwa

In the hot summer evenings, when the grassy patches around the lakes and rivers sparkle with fireflies, the Indians sing a song to them.

Flitting white-fire-bug,
Flitting white-fire-bug,
Give me your light before I go to sleep.
Give me your light before I go to sleep.
Come, little waving fire-bug.
Come, little waving fire-bug.
Light me with your bright torch.
Light me with your bright torch.*

* Saw the fire-fly, Wah-wah-taysee,
Flitting through the dusk of evening,
With the twinkle of its candle,
Lighting up the brakes and bushes;
And he sang the song of children,
Sang the song Nokomis taught him;
"Wah-wah-taysee, little fire-fly,
Little, flitting, white-fire insect . . ."

—*Hiawatha*

SONG OF THE MOTHER BEARS

Cherokee

One day a hunter in the woods heard singing in a cave. He came near and peeped in. It was a mother bear singing to her cubs and telling them what to do when the hunters came after them.

Mother Bear said,

When you hear the hunter
    coming down the creek, then
Tsagi, tsagi, hwilahi
Tsagi, tsagi, hwilahi,
Upstream, upstream, you must go.
Upstream, upstream, you must go.

But if you hear them coming down stream,
Ge-i, ge-i, hwilahi,
Ge-i, ge-i, hwilahi,
Downstream, downstream, you must go.
Downstream, downstream, you must go.

Another hunter out in the woods one day thought he heard a woman singing to a baby. He followed the sound up a creek until he came to a cave under the bushes. Inside there was a mother bear rocking her cub in her paws and singing to it,

Let me carry you on my back,
Let me carry you on my back,
Let me carry you on my back,

Let me carry you on my back,
Let me carry you on my back,
On the sunny side go to sleep.
On the sunny side go to sleep.

This was after some of the people had become bears. The hunter knew they were of the Ani Tsagulin tribe.*

THE MAN IN THE STUMP

Cherokee

An Indian had a field of corn ripening in the sun. One day when he wanted to look at it, he climbed a stump. Now the stump was hollow and in it was a nest of bear cubs. The man slipped and fell down upon the cubs.

At once the cubs began calling for their mother, and Mother Bear came running. She began to climb down into the stump backwards. Then the Indian caught hold of her leg; thus she became frightened. She began to climb out and dragged the Indian also to the top of the stump. Thus he got out of the stump.

* See "Origin of the Bear."

THE ANTS AND THE KATYDIDS

Biloxi

The Ancient of Ants was building a house. She worked hard to finish her house before the cold weather came.

Now when it was very cold, the Katydid and the Locust reached her house, asking for shelter. They said they had no houses.

The Ancient of Ants scolded them. She said, "After you are grown up, in the warm weather, you sing all the time, instead of building a house." She would not let them come into her house.

Then the Katydid and the Locust were ashamed, and as the weather was very cold, they died. That is why katydids and locusts die every winter, while the ants live in their warm houses. But the katydids and locusts never do anything in warm weather but sing.

WHEN THE OWL MARRIED

Cherokee

Once there was a widow with only one daughter. She said often, "You should marry and then there will be a man to go hunting."

Then one day a man came courting the daughter. He said, "Will you marry me?"

The girl said, "I can only marry a good worker. We need a man who is a good hunter and who will work in the cornfield."

"I am exactly that sort of a man," he said. So the mother said they might marry.

Then the next morning the mother gave the man a hoe. She said, "Go, hoe the corn. When breakfast is ready I will call you." Then she went to call him. She followed a sound as of someone hoeing on stony soil. When she reached the place, there was only a small circle of hoed ground. Over in the thicket someone said, "Hoo-hoo!"

When the man came back in the evening, the mother said, "Where have you been all day?"

He said, "Hard at work."

The mother said, "I couldn't find you."

"I was over in the thicket cutting sticks to mark off the field," he said.

"But you did not come to the lodge to eat at all," she answered.

"I was too busy," he said.

Early the next morning he started off with his hoe over his shoulder.

Then the mother went again to call him, when the meal was ready. The hoe was lying there, but there was no sign of work done. And away over in the thicket, she heard a hu-hu calling, *Sau-h! sau-h! sau-h! hoo-hoo! hoo-hoo! hoo-hoo! chi! chi! chi! whew!*

Now when the man came home that night, the mother asked, "What have you been doing all day?"

"Working hard," he said.

"But you were not there when I came after you."

"Oh, I went over in the thicket awhile," said the man, "to see some of my relatives."

Then the mother said, "I have lived here a long while, and no one lives in that swamp but lazy hu-hus. My daughter wants a husband that can work and not a hu-hu!" And she drove him from the house.

PART FOUR

Eagle · Panther · Opossum

THE KITE AND THE EAGLE

Kite was very boastful. One day he spoke scornfully of Eagle, who heard his words. Kite began to sing in a loud voice,

> I alone,
> I alone,
> Can go up,
> So as to seem as if hanging from the blue sky.

Eagle answered scornfully. He sang,

> Who is this,
> Who is this,
> Who boasts of flying so high?

Kite was ashamed. He answered in a small voice, "Oh, I was only singing of the great Khakate. It is he who is said to fly so high."

Eagle answered, "Oh you crooked tongue! You are below my notice."

Then Eagle soared high into the sky. But just as soon as he was out of hearing, Kite began to sing again in a very loud voice,

> I alone,
> I alone,
> Can go up,
> So as to seem as if hanging from the blue sky.

THE LINNET AND THE EAGLE

Ojibwa

All the Birds met in council, each claiming to fly the highest. Each one claimed to be the chief. Therefore the council decided that each bird should fly toward the Sky-land.

Some of the birds flew very swiftly; but they tired and flew back to earth. Now Eagle went far above all. When Eagle could fly no farther, Linnet, who had perched upon Eagle's back, flew up. Far above Eagle flew the tiny gray bird.

Now when the Birds held a council again, Eagle was made chief. Eagle had flown higher than all the rest, and had carried Linnet on his back.

HOW PARTRIDGE GOT HIS WHISTLE

Cherokee

In the old days, Terrapin had a fine whistle and Partridge had none. Terrapin whistled constantly. He was always boasting of his fine whistle.

One day Partridge said, "Let me try your whistle."

Terrapin said, "No." He was afraid Partridge would try some trick.

Partridge said, "Oh, if you are afraid, stay right here while I use it."

So Terrapin gave it to him. Partridge strutted around, whistling constantly.

He said, "How does it sound with me?"

"You do it very well," said Terrapin, walking by his side.

"Now how do you like it?" asked Partridge, running ahead.

"It's fine," said Terrapin, trying to keep up with him. "But don't run so fast!"

"How do you like it now?" asked Partridge, spreading his wings and flying to a tree top. Terrapin could only look up at him.

Partridge never gave the whistle back. He has it even to this day. And Terrapin was so ashamed because Partridge stole his whistle, and Turkey had stolen his scalp, that he shuts himself up in his box whenever anyone comes near him.

HOW KINGFISHER GOT HIS BILL

Cherokee

Some of the old men say that Kingfisher was meant in the beginning to be a water bird, but because he had no web on his feet and not a good bill, he could not get enough to eat. The animals knew of this, so they held a council. Afterwards they made him a bill like a long, sharp awl. This fish gig he was to use spearing fish. When they fastened it onto his mouth, he flew first to the top of a tree. Then he darted down into the water and came up with a fish on his bill. And ever since, Kingfisher has been the best fisherman.

But some of the old people say it was this way.

Blacksnake found Yellowhammer's nest in the hollow tree and killed all the young birds. Yellowhammer at once went to the Little People for help. They sent her to Kingfisher. So she went on to him.

Kingfisher came at once, and after flying back and forth past the hole in the hollow tree, he made a quick dart at the snake and pulled him out, dead. When they looked, they saw he had pierced Blacksnake with a slender fish he carried in his bill. Therefore the Little People said he would make good use of a spear, so they gave him his long bill.

WHY THE BLACKBIRD HAS RED WINGS

Chitimacha

One day an Indian became so angry with everyone that he set the sea marshes on fire because he wanted to burn up the world.

A little blackbird saw it. He flew up into a tree and shouted, "*Ku nam wi cu! Ku nam wi cu!* The world and all is going to burn."

The man said, "If you do not go away, I will kill you." But the bird only kept shouting, "*Ku nam wi cu!* The world and all is going to burn."

Then the Indian threw a shell and hit the little bird on the wings, making them bleed. That is how the red-winged blackbird came by its red wings.

Now when people saw the marshes burning, they quickly ran down and killed game which had been driven from it by the fire. Then they said to the angry man, "Because you put fire in those tall weeds, the deer and bear and other animals have been driven out and we have killed them. You have aided us by burning them."

Nowadays when the red-winged blackbird comes around the house, he still shouts, "*Ku nam wi cu,*" so they say.

BALL GAME OF THE BIRDS AND ANIMALS

Cherokee

Once the Animals challenged the Birds to a great ball play, and the Birds accepted. The Animals met near the river, in a smooth grassy field. The Birds met in the tree top over by the ridge.

Now the leader of the Animals was Bear. He was very strong and heavy. All the way to the river he tossed up big logs to show his strength and boasted of how he would win against the Birds. Terrapin was with the Animals. He was not the little terrapin we have now, but the first Terrapin. His shell was so hard the heaviest blows could not hurt him, and he was very large. On the way to the river he rose on his hind feet and dropped heavily again. He did this many times, bragging that thus he would crush any bird that tried to take the ball from him. Then there was Deer, who could outrun all the others. And there were many other animals.

Now the leader of the Birds was Eagle; and also Hawk, and the great Tlanuwa. They were all swift and strong of flight.

Now first they had a ball dance. Then after the dance, as the birds sat in the trees, two tiny little animals no larger than field mice climbed up the tree where Eagle sat. They crept out to the branch tips to Eagle.

They said, "We wish to play ball."

Eagle looked at them. They were four-footed. He said, "Why don't you join the Animals? You belong there."

"The Animals make fun of us," they said. "They drive us away because we are small."

Eagle pitied them. He said, "But you have no wings."

Then at once Eagle and Hawk and all the Birds held a council in the trees. At last they said to the little fellows, "We will make wings for you."

But they could not think just how to do it. Then a Bird said, "The head of our drum is made of groundhog skin. Let us make wings from that." So they took two pieces of leather from the drum and shaped them for wings. They stretched them with cane splints and fastened them on the forelegs of one of the little animals. So they made Tlameha, the Bat. They began to teach him.

First they threw the ball to him. Bat dropped and circled about in the air on his new wings. He did not let the ball drop. The Birds saw at once he would be one of their best men.

Now they wished to give wings also to the second little animal, but there was no more leather. And there was no more time. Then somebody said they might make wings for the other man by stretching his skin. Therefore two large birds took hold from opposite sides with their strong bills. Thus they stretched his skin. Thus they made Tewa, the Flying Squirrel.

Then Eagle threw to him the ball. At once Flying Squirrel sprang after it, caught it in his teeth, and carried it through the air to another tree nearby.

Then the game began. Almost at the first toss, Flying Squirrel caught the ball and carried it up a tree. Then he threw it to the Birds, who kept it in the air for some time.

When it dropped to the earth, Bear rushed to get it, but Martin darted after it and threw it to Bat, who was flying near the ground. Bat doubled and dodged with the ball, and kept it out of the way of Deer. At last Bat threw it between the posts. So the Birds won the game.

Bear and Terrapin, who had boasted of what they would do, never had a chance to touch the ball.

Because Martin saved the ball when it dropped to the ground, the Birds afterwards gave him a gourd in which to build his nest. He still has it.

WHY THE BIRDS HAVE SHARP TAILS

Biloxi

Once upon a time, they say, the world turned over. Then the waters rose very high and many people died. A woman took two children and lodged in a tree. She sat there waiting for the waters to sink, for she had no way of reaching the ground.

When the woman saw the Ancient of Red-headed Buzzards, she called to him, "Help me to get down and I will give you one of the children." He assisted her, but she did not give him the child.

The waters were so deep that the birds were clinging by their claws to the clouds, but their tails were under water. That is why their tails are always sharp. One of these birds was the Ancient of Yellowhammers. Therefore its tailfeathers are sharp at the ends. The large Red-headed Woodpecker was there, too, and the Ivory-billed Woodpecker, and that is why their tails have their present shape.

THE WILDCAT AND THE TURKEYS

Biloxi

The Ancient of Wildcats had been creeping up on the Wild Turkeys trying to catch some. He tried in vain. Then he got a bag, crawled inside, and rolled himself along. He rolled himself to the Ancient of Turkey Gobblers.

Wildcat said, "Get into my bag and see what fun it is to roll."

The Ancient of Turkey Gobblers crawled into the bag. Wildcat tied up the end and rolled it along for some time. After he had rolled it quite a distance, he stopped and untied the bag.

"It is very good," said the First of All the Turkey Gobblers. Then he said to the other Wild Turkeys, "Get in the bag and see how pleasant it is."

But the young Turkeys were afraid. Gobbler urged them to try the new game. At last one young Turkey stepped into the bag. Wildcat tied the end and pretended that he was going to roll it. It would not go.

"It will not go because it is too light. There is only one in it," said Wildcat. "Let another young Turkey step in."

At last another young Turkey stepped in. Wildcat tied the bag, threw it over his shoulder, and ran home. When he reached home he laid the bag down.

Then Wildcat said to his mother, "I have brought home something on my back, and placed it outside. Beware lest you untie the bag."

His mother said to herself, "I wonder what it can be." So she untied the bag. One of the Turkeys flew out. She managed to catch the other one. She caught both feet with one hand, and both wings with the other. She cried out, "Help! Help! I have caught four!"

The Ancient of Wildcats scolded his mother. Then he killed the Turkey and cooked it. His mother went into another room.

Then Wildcat spread his feast. As he was eating the Turkey he made a constant noise. He walked back and forth. He talked continually and kept up a steady rattling. When he stopped the noise a little he said, "I am going home," as if a guest were speaking. He said this again and again. He made a noise with his feet as if people were walking about. He ate all the Turkey except the hip bone.

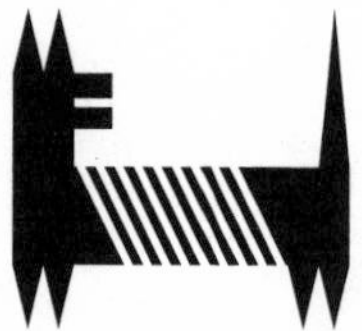

THE BRANT AND THE OTTER

Biloxi

Once upon a time the Ancient of Brants and the Ancient of Otters were living as friends. One day the Ancient of Otters said to the Ancient of Brants, "Come to see me tomorrow," and departed.

Brant went to make the call. When he arrived, the Ancient of Otters said, "Halloo! I have nothing at all for you to eat! Sit down!" Then he went fishing. He used a "leather vine" which he jerked now and then to straighten it. He caught many fish. When he reached home he cooked them.

When the fish were cooked, ready for the feast, the Ancient of Otters put some into a very flat dish. But the Ancient of Brants could not eat from a flat dish. All he could do was to hit his bill against the dish, and raise his head as if swallowing something. But Otter ate rapidly.

Otter said to his guest, "Have you eaten enough?"

"Yes, I am satisfied," said Brant.

"No, you are not satisfied," said Otter. He took more fish and placed them in the flat dish, eating rapidly as before. Brant could only hit his bill against the side of the dish.

When the Ancient of Brants was departing, he said to Otter, "Come to see me tomorrow."

When Otter reached the house of the Ancient of Brants the next day, Brant cried, "Halloo! I have nothing at all to give you to eat! Sit down!"

Then the Ancient of Brants went fishing, using a "leather vine" which he jerked now and then to straighten it. He caught many fish and took them home to cook them. When the fish were cooked, they began to feast. But the Ancient of Brants had put some into a small round dish. Ancient of Otters could not get his mouth into the dish. But Brant ate rapidly.

"Have you eaten enough?" Brant asked, after a while.

Otter replied, "Yes, I am satisfied."

"Nonsense!" said the Ancient of Brants. "How could you possibly be satisfied! I have served you as you served me."

But this ended their friendship.

THE TINY FROG AND THE PANTHER

Biloxi

The Ancient of Tiny Frogs* was shut up by his grandmother, so that he might learn magic. Then she took him on a journey.

First they met the Ancient of Panthers. The grandmother said to him, "This is your sister's son. Look at him and wrestle with him." The Ancient of Panthers was very brave. To show his strength, he climbed very high up a tree which he tore to pieces, falling to the ground with it.

Then he seized the Ancient of Tiny Frogs. But the frog caught him by the hind legs and whipped him against a tree. He beat him so severely that Panther's jaw was broken in many places. That is why all panthers have a short jaw.

The Ancient of Tiny Frogs and his grandmother continued their journey. Next they met Bear. The grandmother said to him, "Look at your sister's son. Go and wrestle with him." Bear began to pull the limbs off a tree to show his strength. Soon he rushed upon the Ancient of Tiny Frogs. But that one caught Bear by the hind legs and beat him against a tree until he broke off short his tail. That is why bears have such very short tails.

Again the old grandmother, singing as she

* The tiny frog, called péska, is a black one, not more than an inch long, living in muddy streams in Louisiana. It differs from the bullfrog, common frog, and tree frog.

walked, went along the trail with her grandson. They met Buffalo. She said, "Look at your sister's son. Go and wrestle with him." Now Buffalo was very strong. With his horns he uprooted a tree, and then spent some moments in breaking it to pieces. Then he rushed at the Ancient of Tiny Frogs. But that one caught Buffalo by the hind legs and beat him against a tree. He beat him until the back of his neck was broken and he had a great hump on his shoulders. So Buffalo went away, but that is why buffaloes have such very heavy, humpbacked shoulders.

Again they walked along the trail, singing. It was not long before they met with Deer. To him the grandmother said, "Look at your sister's son. Go and wrestle with him." Deer leaped up to show his agility. Then he sprang at the Ancient of Tiny Frogs. But that one seized him by the legs and beat him against a tree, breaking his nose, and leaving him with a very small nose, even as deer today have small noses.

Then the Ancient of Tiny Frogs said to Deer: "I shall remain here under the leaves. When hunters are after you and have almost reached you, I will urge you to escape by saying, "*Pés! Pés!* When I say that, do your best to get away."

Hardly had he finished speaking, when he cried out, "*Pés! Pés!* It is so! Go quickly! Do your best!" Then Deer leaped away. For just then the hunters had come, sure enough.

Therefore, when a tiny frog cries out now, people say that some one is on the point of running after a deer.

THE FRIGHTENER OF HUNTERS

Choctaw (Bayou Lacomb)

Kashehotapalo is the frightener of hunters. His head is small and dried up, like an old man's. His legs and feet are like those of a deer. He lives in low, swampy places, far away from men.

If the hunters come near him, when they are chasing a deer, he slips up behind them and calls loudly. Thus he frightens them away. His voice is like that of a woman. His name means "the woman call."

THE HUNTER AND THE ALLIGATOR

Choctaw (Bayou Lacomb)

All the hunters in a village killed many deer one winter, except one man. This one saw many deer. Sometimes he drew his bow and shot at them; yet they escaped.

Now this hunter had been away from his village three days. He had seen many deer; not one had he killed. On the third day, when the sun was hot over his head, he saw an alligator.

Alligator was in a dry, sandy spot. He had had no water for many days. He was dry and shriveled.

Alligator said to the hunter, "Where can water be found?" The hunter said, "In that forest, not far away, is cold water."

"I cannot go there alone," said Alligator. "Come nearer. Do not fear." The hunter went nearer, but he was afraid.

"You are a hunter," said Alligator, "but all the deer escape you. Carry me into the water, and I will make you a great hunter. You shall kill many deer."

The hunter was still afraid. Then he said, "I will carry you, but first I must bind you so that you cannot scratch me; and your mouth, so that you cannot bite me."

So Alligator rolled over on his back and let the hunter bind him. He fastened his legs and mouth firmly. Then he carried Alligator on his shoulders to the water in the forest. He unfastened the cords and threw him in.

Alligator came to the surface three times. He said, "Take your bow and arrow and go into the woods. You will find a small doe. Do not kill it. Then you will find a large doe. Do not kill it. You will meet a small buck. Do not kill that. Then you will meet a large, old buck. Kill that."

The hunter took his bow and arrow. Everything happened just as Alligator had foretold. Then he killed the large, old buck. So he became a very great hunter. There was always venison in his wigwam.

THE GROUNDHOG DANCE

Cherokee

Seven wolves once caught a groundhog. They said, "Now we'll kill you and have something to eat."

Groundhog said, "When we find good food, we should rejoice over it, as people do in the green-corn dances. You will kill me, and I cannot help myself. But if you want to dance, I'll sing for you. Now this is a new dance. I will lean up against seven trees in turn. You will dance forward and then go back. At the last turn you may kill me."

Now the Wolves were very hungry, but they wanted to learn the new dance. Groundhog leaned up against a tree and began to sing. He sang,

Ho wi ye a hi

and all the Wolves danced forward. When he shouted *"Yu!"* they turned and danced back in line.

"That's fine," said Groundhog, after the first dance was over. Then he went to the next tree and began the second song. He sang,

Hi ya yu we,

and the Wolves danced forward. When he shouted *"Yu!"* they danced back in a straight line.

At each song, Groundhog took another tree, getting closer and closer to his hole under a stump. At the seventh song, Groundhog said,

"Now this is the last dance. When I shout *'Yu!'* all come after me. The one who gets me may have me."

Then he sang a long time, until the Wolves were at quite a distance in a straight line. Then he shouted *"Yu!"* and darted for his hole.

At once the Wolves turned and were after him. The foremost Wolf caught his tail and gave it such a jerk he broke it off. That is why Groundhog has such a short tail.

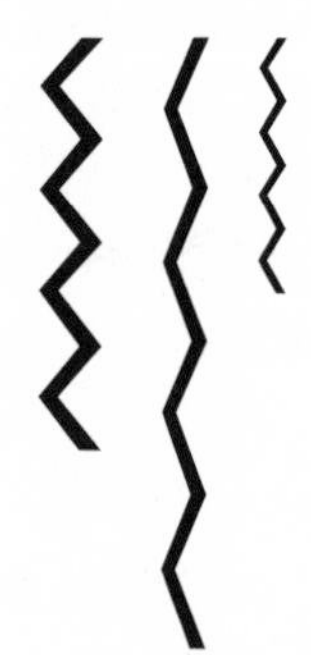

THE RACOON

Menomini

One day Racoon went into the woods to fast and dream. He dreamed that someone said to him, "When you awaken, paint your face and body with bands of black and white. That will be your own."

When Racoon awoke, he painted himself as he had been told to do. So we see him, even to the present day.

WHY THE OPOSSUM PLAYS DEAD

Biloxi

The Ancient of Opossums thought that he would reach a certain pond very early in the morning, so that he might catch the crawfish on the shore. But someone else reached there first, and when Opossum reached there the crawfish were all gone.

This person did this every day. Opossum did not know who it was, so he lay in wait for him. He found it was the Ancient of Racoons.

They argued about the crawfish and the pond. They agreed to see which could rise the earlier in the morning, go around the shore of the pond, and catch the crawfish.

Racoon said, "I rise very early. I never sleep until daylight comes."

Opossum said the same thing. Then each went home.

Now Opossum lay down in a hollow tree and slept there a long time. He arose when the sun was very high and went to the pond. But Racoon had been there ahead of him, and had eaten all the crawfish. Racoon sang the Song of the Racoon as he was going home. Opossum stood listening. He, too, sang. He sang the Song of the Opossum, thus:

Hí na kí-yu wus-sé-di

He met the Racoon who had eaten all the crawfish.

"Ha!" said Racoon. "I have been eating very long, and I was going home, as I was sleepy."

Opossum said, "I, too, have been eating so long that I am sleepy, so I am going home."

Opossum was always telling a lie. People say this of the Opossum because if one hits that animal and throws it down for dead, soon it gets up and walks off.

WHY THE 'POSSUM'S TAIL IS BARE

Cherokee

'Possum used to have a long, bushy tail and he was so proud of it that he combed it out every morning and sang about it at the dance. Now Rabbit had had no tail since Bear pulled it off because he was jealous. Therefore he planned to play a trick on 'Possum.

The animals called a great council. They planned to have a dance. It was Rabbit's business to send out the news. One day as he was passing 'Possum's house, he stopped to talk.

"Are you going to the council?" he asked.

"Yes, if I can have a special seat," said 'Possum. "I have such a handsome tail I ought to sit where everyone can see me."

Rabbit said, "I will see that you have a special seat. And I will send someone to comb your tail for the dance." 'Possum was very much pleased.

Rabbit at once went to Cricket, who is an expert hair cutter; therefore the Indians call him the barber. He told Cricket to go the next morning and comb 'Possum's tail for the dance. He told Cricket just what to do.

In the morning, Cricket went to 'Possum's house. 'Possum stretched himself out on the floor and went to sleep, while Cricket combed out his tail and wrapped a red string around it to keep it smooth until night. But all the time, as he wound the string around, he was snipping off the hair closely. 'Possum did not know it.

When it was night, 'Possum went to the council and took his special seat. When it was his turn to dance, he loosened the red string from his tail and stepped into the middle of the lodge.

The drummers began to beat the drum. 'Possum began to sing, "See my beautiful tail."

Every man shouted and 'Possum danced around the circle again, singing, "See what a fine color it has." They all shouted again, and 'Possum went on dancing, as he sang, "See how it sweeps the ground."

Then the animals all shouted so that 'Possum wondered what it meant. He looked around. Every man was laughing at him. Then he looked down at his beautiful tail. It was as bare as a lizard's tail. There was not a hair on it.

He was so astonished and ashamed that he could not say a word. He rolled over on the ground and grinned, just as he does today when taken by surprise.

WHY 'POSSUM HAS A LARGE MOUTH

Choctaw (Bayou Lacomb)

Very little food there was for Deer one dry season. He became thin and weak. One day he met 'Possum. Deer at once exclaimed, "Why, 'Possum, how fat you are! How do you keep so fat when I cannot find enough to eat?"

'Possum said, "I live on persimmons. They are very large this year, so I have all I want to eat."

"How do you get the persimmons?" asked Deer. "They grow so high!"

"That is easy," said 'Possum. "I go to the top of a high hill. Then I run down and strike a persimmon tree so hard with my head that all the ripe persimmons drop on the ground. Then I sit there and eat them."

"That is easily done," said Deer. "I will try it. Now watch me."

'Possum waited. Deer went to the top of a nearby hill. He ran down and struck the tree with his head. 'Possum watched him, laughing. He opened his mouth so wide while he laughed that he stretched it. That is why 'Possum has such a large mouth.

THE PORCUPINE AND THE TWO SISTERS

Menomini

Once there dwelt in a village two sisters, who were the swiftest runners in the Menomini tribe. Towards the setting sun was another village, two days' walk away.

The sisters wished to visit this village. They began to run at great speed. At noon they came to a hollow tree lying across the trail. In the snow on the ground, there, behold! lay the trail of Porcupine, leading to the hollow tree. One of them broke off a stick and began to poke into the log, that Porcupine might come out. She said, "Let's have some fun with him."

"No," said the other sister, "he is a manito. We should leave him alone."

But the girl with a stick poked into the hollow log until Porcupine came out. Then she caught him and pulled out his long quills and threw them in the snow. The other said, "No, it is cold. Porcupine will need his robe."

At last the sisters ran on. The village was still far away.

Now when they left Porcupine, he crawled up a tall pine tree until he reached the very top. Then he faced the north and began to shake his small rattle, singing in time to its sound.

Soon the sky darkened. Snow began to fall. Now the sisters could not run rapidly because of the deepening snow.

One looked back and saw Porcupine in the tree top, shaking his rattle. She said, "We must go back to our own village. I am afraid some harm will overtake us."

The other answered, "No, let us go on. We need not fear Porcupine." The snow became deeper, so they rolled up their blankets as they ran on.

When the sun followed the trail over the edge of the world, the sisters could not even see the village. Still they ran on. Then in the late evening they came to a stream which they knew was near the village.

Behold! It was dark. The snow was very deep. The sisters no longer had strength. They could hear voices in the village. They could not call loud enough to be heard. Thus they perished in the snow.

One should never harm Porcupine because he is a manito.

THE WOLF AND THE DOG

Cherokee

In the beginning, so they say, Dog was put on the mountain side and Wolf beside the fire. When winter came, Dog could not stand the cold, and drove Wolf away from the fire. Wolf ran into the mountains and he liked it so well that he has stayed there ever since.

THE CATFISH AND THE MOOSE

Menomini

Once when the Catfish were all together in one place in the water, the Catfish chief said, "I have often seen a moose come to the edge of the water to eat grass. Let us watch for him and kill him and eat him. He always comes when the sun is a little way up in the sky."

The Catfish agreed to attack Moose. So they went to watch. They crept everywhere in among the grass and rushes when Moose came down to the water's edge, slowly picking at the grass. All the tribe watched to see what the Catfish chief would do. He slipped slowly through the marshy grass to where Moose was standing. He thrust his spear into Moose's leg.

Moose said, "Who has thrust a spear into my leg?" He looked down and saw the Catfish tribe. At once he began to trample upon them with his hoofs. He killed many, but others escaped and swam down the river.

Catfish still carry spears, but their heads are flat, because Moose tramped them down in the mud.

TURTLE

Menomini

There was a large camp in which Miqkano, the Turtle, took up his abode. He built a wigwam but he had no one to keep house for him. He thought he needed a wife.

Now Turtle found a young woman whom he liked. He said, "I want you to be my wife."

She said. "How are you going to provide for me? You cannot keep up with the rest of the people when they move."

Turtle replied, "I can keep up with the best of your people."

Then the young woman wanted to put him off. She said, "Oh, well, I will marry you in the spring."

Turtle was vexed with this. At last he said, "I shall go to war and take some captives. When I return in the spring, I shall expect you to marry me."

Then Turtle prepared to go on the war path. He called all his friends, the Turtles, to him. He left camp, followed by a throng of curious Indians. The young woman he wanted to marry laughed as the Turtles moved away. They were so very slow.

Turtle was vexed again. He said, "In four days from now you will surely mourn for me because I shall be at a great distance from you."

"Why," said the girl, laughing, "In four days from this time you will scarcely be out of sight."

Turtle immediately corrected himself, and said, "I did not mean four days, but four years. Then I shall return."

Now the Turtles started off. They traveled slowly on until one day they found a great tree lying across their trail.

Turtle said, "This we cannot pass unless we go around it. That would take too long. What shall we do?"

Some said, "Let us burn a hole through the trunk," but in this they did not succeed.

Therefore they had to turn back home, but it was a long time before they came near the Indian village again. They wanted to appear as successful warriors, so as they came near, they set up the war song. The Indians heard them. They at once ran out to see the scalps and the spoils. But when they came near, the Turtles each seized an Indian by the arm and said, "We take you our prisoners. You are our spoils."

The Indians who were captured in this way were very angry. Now the Turtle chief had captured the young woman he said he was going to marry. He said to the Indian girl, "Now that I have you I will keep you."

Now it was necessary to organize a dance to celebrate the victory over the Indians. Everyone dressed in his best robe and beads. Turtle sang, "Whoever comes near me will die, will die, will die!" and the others danced around him in a circle. At once the Indians became alarmed. Each one fled to his own lodge, in the village. Turtle also went to the village, but he arrived much later because he could not travel so fast.

Someone said to him, "That girl has married another man."

"Is that true?" stormed Turtle. "Let me see the man."

So he went to that wigwam. He called, "I am going for the woman who promised to be my wife."

Her husband said, "Here comes Turtle. Now what is to be done?"

"I shall take care of that," said his wife.

Turtle came in and seized her. He said, "Come along with me. You belong to me."

She pulled back. She said, "You broke your promise." The husband said also, "Yes, you promised to go to war and bring back some prisoners. You failed to do so."

Turtle said, "I did go. I returned with many prisoners." Then he picked up the young woman and carried her off.

Now when Turtle arrived at his own wigwam, the young woman went at once to a friend and borrowed a large kettle. She filled it with water and set it on to boil. Turtle became afraid. He said, "What are you doing?"

She said, "I am heating some water. Do you know how to swim?"

"Oh, yes," said Turtle. "I can swim."

The young woman said, "You jump in the water and swim. I can wash your shell."

So Turtle tried to swim in the hot water. Then the other Turtles, seeing their chief swimming in the kettle, climbed over the edge and jumped into the water. Thus Turtle and his warriors were conquered.

PART FIVE

Sun · Moon · Stars

THE WORSHIP OF THE SUN

Ojibwa

Long ago, an Ojibwa Indian and his wife lived on the shores of Lake Huron. They had one son, who was named "O-na-wut-a-qui-o, He-that-catches-the-clouds."

Now the boy was very handsome, and his parents thought highly of him, but he refused to make the fast of his tribe. His father gave him charcoal; yet he would not blacken his face. They refused him food; but he wandered along the shore, and ate the eggs of birds. One day his father took from him by force the eggs of the birds. He took them violently. Then he threw charcoal to him. Then did the boy blacken his face and begin his fast.

Now he fell asleep. A beautiful woman came down through the air and stood beside him. She said, "I have come for you. Step in my trail."

At once he began to rise through the air. They passed through an opening in the sky, and he found himself on the Sky-plain. There were flowers on the beautiful plain, and streams of fresh, cold water. The valleys were green and fair. Birds were singing. The Sky-land was very beautiful.

There was but one lodge, and it was divided into two parts. In one end were bright and glowing robes, spears, and bows and arrows. At the other end, the garments of a woman were hung.

The woman said, "My brother is coming and I must hide you." So she put him in a corner and spread over him a broad, shining belt. When the brother came in, he was very richly dressed, and glowing. He took down his great pipe and his tobacco.

At last, he said, "Nemissa, my elder sister, when will you end these doings? The Greatest of Spirits has commanded that you should not take away the children of earth. I know of the coming of O-na-wut-a-qui-o." Then he called out, "Come out of your hiding. You will get hungry if you remain there." When the boy came out, he gave him a handsome pipe of red sandstone, and a bow and arrows.

So the boy stayed in the Sky-land. But soon he found that every morning, very early, the brother left the wigwam. He returned in the evening, and then the sister left it and was gone all night. One day he said to the brother, "Let me go with you." "Yes," said the brother, and the next morning they started off.

The two traveled a long while over a smooth plain. It was a very long journey. He became hungry. At last he said, "Is there no game?"

"Wait until we reach the place where I always stop to eat," said the brother. So they journeyed on. At last they came to a place spread over with fine mats. It was near a hole in the Sky-plain.

The Indian looked down through the hole. Below were great lakes and the villages of his people. He could see in one place feasting and dancing, and in another a war party silently stealing upon the enemy. In a green plain young warriors were playing ball.

The brother said, "Do you see those children?" and he sent a dart down from the Sky-plain. At once a little boy fell to the ground. Then all the people gathered about the lodge of his father. The Indian, looking down through the hole, could hear the *she-she-gwan* of the *meta,* and the loud singing. Then Sun, the brother, called down, "Send me up a white dog."

Immediately a white dog was killed by the medicine men, and roasted, because the child's father ordered a feast. All the wise men and the medicine men were there.

Sun said to the Indian, "Their ears are open and they listen to my voice."

Now the Indians on the Earth-plain divided the dog, and placed pieces on the bark for those who were at the feast. Then the master of the feast called up, "We send this to thee, Great Manito." At once the roasted dog came up to Sun in the Sky-plain. Thus Sun and the Indian had food. Then Sun healed the boy whom he had struck down. Then he began again to travel along the trail in the Sky-plain, and they reached their wigwam by another road.

Then O-na-wut-a-qui-o began to weary of the Sky-land. At last he said to Moon, "I wish to go home."

Moon said, "Since you like better the care and poverty of the earth, you may return. I will take you back."

At once the Indian youth awoke. He was in the very plain where he had fallen asleep after he had blackened his face and begun his fast. But his mother said he had been gone a year.

TASHKA AND WALO

Choctaw (Bayou Lacomb)

Tashka and Walo were brothers. They lived a long while ago, so they say. Every morning they saw Sun come up over the edge of the earth. Then he followed the trail through the sky.

When they were four years old, they started to follow Sun's trail. They walked all day, but that night when Sun died, they were still in their own country. They knew all the hills and rivers. Then they slept.

Next morning they began again to follow Sun, but when he died at the edge of the earth, they could still see their own land.

Then they followed Sun many years. At last they became grown men.

One day they reached a great sea-water. There was no land except the shore on which they stood. When Sun went down over the edge of the earth that day, they saw him sink into the waters. Then they crossed the sea-water, to the edge. So they came to Sun's home.

All around there were many women. The stars are women, and Moon also. Moon is Sun's wife.

Moon asked them how they had found their way. They were very far from their own land. They said, "For many years we have followed Sun's trail."

Sun said, "Do you know your way home?" They said, "No." So Sun took them up to the edge of the water. They could see the earth, but they could not see their own land.

Sun asked, "Why did you follow me?" They said, "We wished to see where you lived."

Sun said, "I will send you home. But for four days you must not speak a word to any person. If you do not speak, you shall live long. You shall have much wealth."

Then Sun called to Buzzard. He put the two brothers on Buzzard's back. He said, "Take them back to earth." So Buzzard started for the earth.

Now the clouds are halfway between heaven and earth. The wind never blows above the clouds, so they say.

Buzzard flew from heaven to the clouds. The brothers could easily keep their hold. Then Buzzard flew from the clouds to the earth. But now Wind blew them in all directions. Then at last they came to earth. They saw the trees around their own village. They rested under the trees. An old man passing by knew them. So he went down the trail and told their mother. She at once hastened to see them. When she met them she began to talk. She made them talk to her. They told her. So they spoke before the four days were ended. Therefore Sun could not keep his promise.

SUN AND MOON

Menomini

Once upon a time, Ke-so, the Sun, and his sister, Tipa-ke-so, the Moon, the "last-night sun," lived together in a wigwam in the East. One day Sun dressed himself to go hunting, took his bows and arrows, and left. He was gone a long time. When he did not return, his sister became frightened, and came out into the sky to look for her brother. At last he returned, bringing with him a bear which he had shot.

Moon still comes up into the sky and travels for twenty days. Then she disappears, and for four days nothing is seen of her. At the end of the four days, she comes into the sky again, and travels twenty days more.

Sun is a being like ourselves. He wears an otter skin about his head.

THE MOON PERSON

Biloxi

In olden days, the Moon Person used to make visits to the Indians. One day a child put out a dirty little hand and made a black spot on Moon Person. Therefore Moon felt ashamed and when night came he disappeared. He went up above. He stays up above all the time now, so they say. Sometimes he is dressed altogether in a shining robe, and therefore he is bright at night. But immediately afterwards he disappears. You can still see the black spot, so they say.

THE STAR CREATURES

Cherokee

One night hunters in the mountains noticed two shining lights moving along the top of a distant ridge. After a while the lights vanished on the other side. Thus they watched many nights, talking around the camp fire.

One morning they traveled to the ridge. Then they searched long. At last they found two round creatures covered with soft fur or downy feathers. They had small heads.

Then the hunters took these strange creatures to their camp. They watched them. In the day, they were only balls of gray fur; only when the breeze stirred their fur, then sparks flew out. At night they grew bright and shone like stars.

They kept very quiet. They did not stir, so the hunters did not fasten them. One night they suddenly rose from the ground like balls of fire. They went above the tops of the trees, and then higher until they reached the Skyland. So the hunters knew they were stars.

METEORS

Menomini

When a star falls from the sky it leaves a fiery trail. It does not die. Its shade goes back to its own place to shine again. The Indians sometimes find the small stars where they have fallen in the grass.

THE AURORA BOREALIS

Menomini

In the Land of the North Wind live the *manabaiwok,* the giants of whom our old people tell. The *manabaiwok* are our friends, but we do not see them any more. They are great hunters and fishermen. Whenever they come out with their torches to spear fish, we know it because the sky is bright over that place.

THE WEST WIND

Chitimacha

A little boy named Ustapu was one day lying on the shore of a lake. His people had just reached the shore from the prairies, but the wind was too high for them to cross.

As he lay there, he suddenly saw another boy fanning himself with a fan of turkey wings. This was the boy who made the West Wind. Ustapu said to his tribe, "I can break the arm of the boy who makes West Wind." But they laughed at him. He took a shell and threw it at the boy and struck his left arm.

Therefore when the West Wind is high, the Indians say that the boy is using his strong arm. When the West Wind is a gentle breeze, they say he is using his injured arm. Before that, the West Wind had always been so strong it was very diagreeable, because Wind-maker could use both arms. Now it is much gentler.

The Indians think this boy also made the other winds.

THE LONE LIGHTNING

Ojibwa

At one time an orphan boy whose uncle was very unkind to him ran away. He ran a long way. He ran until night. Then because he was afraid of wild animals, he climbed into a tree in the forest. It was a high pine tree, and he climbed into the forked branches of it.

A person came to him from the upper sky. He said, "Follow me. Step in my trail. I have seen how badly you are treated." Then at once as the boy stepped in his trail, he rose higher and higher into the upper sky. Then the person put twelve arrows into his hands. He said, "There are evil manitoes in the sky. Go to war against them. Shoot them with your bow and arrows."

The boy went into the northern part of the upper sky. Soon he saw a manito and shot at him. But that one's magic was too strong. Therefore the shot failed. There was only a single streak of lightning in the northern sky, yet there was no storm, and not even a cloud.

Eleven times the boy thus failed to kill a manito, and thus he had but one arrow left. He held this in his hands a long while, looking around. Now these evil manitoes had very strong medicine. They could change their form in a moment. But they feared the boy's arrows because they were also strong magic. And because they had been given to him by a good manito, they had power to kill.

At last the boy saw the chief of the evil manitoes. He drew his bow and shot his last arrow; but the chief saw it coming. At once he changed himself into a rock. And the arrow buried itself in a crack of the rock. The chief was very angry. He cried, "Now your arrows are all gone! And because you have dared to shoot at me, you shall become the trail of your arrow."

Thus at once he changed the boy into Nazhik-a-wawa, the Lone Lightning.

THE THUNDERS

Cherokee

The Great Thunder and his sons, the two Thunder boys, live far in the West, above the Sky-plain. The lightning and the rainbow are their beautiful robes. Medicine men pray to Thunder, and call him the Red Man because there is so much red in his dress.

There are other thunders that live lower down, in the cliffs and mountains, and under waterfalls. They travel on bridges from one peak to another, but the Indian cannot see these bridges. The Great Thunders above the sky are kind and helpful when we make medicine to them, but the others are always plotting mischief. One must not point to the rainbow.

MONTHS OF THE YEAR

Natchez

The Natchez begin the year in March, each being a lunar month. Therefore there are thirteen.

1 Deer month

2 Strawberry month

3 Little Corn month

4 Watermelon month

5 Peach month (July)

6 Mulberry month

7 Great Corn month (maize)

8 Turkey month (October)

9 Bison month

10 Bear month

11 Cold meal month (January)

12 Chestnut month

13 Nut month (nuts broken to make bread, at the close of winter, when supplies run low)

WHY THE OAKS AND SUMACHS REDDEN

Fox

Once on a time, long ago, when it was winter, so they say, it snowed for the first time. And while the very first snow lay on the ground, so they say, three men went early in the morning to hunt for game.

In a thick growth of shrub on a side hill, a bear had entered in. They could see the trail in the snow. One went in after him, and started him going in flight.

"Away from The-place-whence-comes-the-cold, he is making fast!" he called to the others.

But the one who had gone round by way of The-place-from-whence-comes-the-cold, cried, "In the direction From-whence-comes-the-source-of-midday is he hurrying away." Thus he said.

The third, who had gone round by way of The-place-whence-comes-the-source-of mid-day, cried out, "Towards The-place-where-the-sun-falls-down is he hastening."

Back and forth for a long while did they keep the bear fleeing from one to another. After a while, one of the hunters who was coming behind looked down. Behold! The earth below was green. For it is really true, so they say, that up into the Sky-land were they led away by the bear. While they were chasing him about the dense growth of shrubs, that was surely the time that up into the Sky-land they went.

Then quickly he called, "Oh, Union-of-rivers, let us turn back. Truly into the Sky-land is he leading us away." So he called to Union-of-rivers, but no answer did he receive from that one.

Now Union-of-rivers, who went running between the man ahead and the man behind, had a little puppy, Hold-tight.

Now in the autumn, they overtook the bear. Then they slew him. After they had slain him, many boughs of an oak did they cut, also of sumach. So with the bear lying on top of the boughs, they skinned him, and cut up the meat. Then they began to scatter the pieces in all directions.

Towards The-place-whence-comes-the-dawn-of-day they hurled the head. In winter, when dawn is nearly breaking, stars appear which are that head, so they say.

Also to the east flung they his backbone. In winter time, certain stars lie close together. These are the backbone, so they say.

And it has also been told of the bear and the hunters that the group of four stars in front are the bear and the three hunters. And between the front star and the star behind, a tiny little star hangs. That is the little dog, Hold-tight, which was the pet of Union-of-rivers.

And so often as autumn comes, the oaks and sumachs redden at the leaf because their boughs were stained with the blood of the bear.

THE MAN OF ICE

Cherokee

Once when the people were burning the woods in the fall, a poplar tree began to burn. It burned until the fire went down into the roots; and then down into the ground. It burned and burned until there was a great hole in the ground, and the people began to be afraid the whole world would burn. They tried to put out the fire, but it was too deep in the ground.

At last someone said, "There is a man living in a house of ice, far toward the Frozen Land. He can put out the fire."

So messengers were sent. They traveled many sleeps until they came to the house of the Man of Ice. He was a little fellow with long braids of hair, hanging to the ground.

He said at once, "Oh, yes, I can help you," and began to unbraid his hair. When it was all loose, he took it in one hand and struck the ends against the other hand. The messengers felt a wind blow against their cheeks.

He struck the ends of his hair again across his hand. A light rain began to fall. A third time he struck the open hand with his hair. Sleet began to fall with rain. The fourth time, and large hailstones fell. They fell as though they came out of the ends of his hair.

"Now go home," said the medicine man. "I shall be there tomorrow."

So the messengers returned. They found the people standing around the burning hole.

The next day, as the people stood again at the burning hole, watching the fire, a light wind came from the north. They were afraid because they knew the medicine man had sent it. The wind made the flames sweep higher. Then a light rain began to fall. It but made the fire hotter. Then came sleet with a heavy rain, and hail. The flames died down but clouds of smoke and steam arose.

Then the people fled to their wigwams for shelter. A great wind arose which blew the hail into the depths of the fire and piled up a great heap of hailstones. Then the fire died out and the smoke ceased.

Now when the people went to look again—a lake stood where flames had been. Yet from below the water came the sound of embers still crackling.

THE NUNNEHI

Cherokee

The Nunnehi are The People Who Live Anywhere. They were spirit people who lived in the highlands of the Cherokee country, and they liked the bald mountain peaks where no timber ever grows.

No one could see the Nunnehi except when the spirit-people let themselves be seen, and then they looked and acted just like other Indians. But they like music and dancing, and hunters in the mountains often could hear the dance songs and the drum; yet when they went towards the sound, it would suddenly shift behind them or in some other direction. They were a friendly people, too. Some Indians have thought they were the same as the Little People; but those are no larger than little children.

Once a boy was with the Nunnehi. When he was about ten or twelve years old, he was playing one day near the river, shooting at a mark with his bow and arrow. Then he started to build a fish trap in the water. While he was piling up the stones in two long walls, a man came and stood on the bank.

The man said, "What are you doing?" The boy told him. The man said, "That's pretty hard work. You ought to rest awhile. Come and take a walk up the river."

The boy said, "No. I am going to the lodge to get something to eat."

"Come to my lodge," said the man. "I'll give you good food and bring you home again in the morning."

So the boy went to the man's lodge with him. They went up the river. The man's wife and all the other people were glad to see him. They gave him plenty to eat. While he was eating, a man that the boy knew very well indeed came and spoke to him. So he did not feel strange.

Afterwards he played with the other children and slept there that night. In the morning, their father took him down the trail. They went down a trail that had a cornfield on one side and a peach orchard on the other, until they came to a cross trail. Then the man said, "Go along this trail across that ridge and you will come to the river road that will take you straight to your home."

So he went back to his house. The boy went down the trail, but soon he turned and looked back. There was no cornfield there; there were no peach trees or house—nothing but trees on the mountain side. Still he was not frightened. He went on until he came to the river trail in sight of his home. He saw many people standing about talking. When they saw him, they ran towards him shouting, "Here he is! He is not drowned or killed in the mountains!

Then they said, "Where have you been? We have been looking for you ever since yesterday noon."

"A man took me over to his house, just across the ridge," said the boy. "I thought Udsi-skala would tell you where I was."

Udsi-skala said, "I have not seen you. I was out all day in my canoe looking for you. It was one of the Nunnehi who made himself look like me."

His mother said, "You say you had plenty to eat there?"

"Yes," said the boy.

"There is no house there," his mother answered. "There is nothing there but trees and rocks, but we hear a drum sometimes in the big bald peak above. The people you saw were the Nunnehi."

THE LITTLE PEOPLE

Cherokee

There is another race of spirits, the Little People. They live in rock caves and in the mountain side. They hardly reach to a man's knee, but they are very handsome, with long hair falling to the ground. They work wonders, and are fond of music. They spend half their time drumming and dancing. If their drum is heard in lonely places in the mountains, it is not safe to follow it. They do not like to be disturbed and they throw a spell over people who annoy them. And even when such a person at last gets back home, he seems dazed.

Sometimes the Little People come near a house at night, but even if people hear them talking, they must not go out. And in the morning, the corn is gathered, or the field cleared, as if a great many people had been at work.

When a hunter finds a knife in the woods, he must say, "Little People, I want to take this," because it may belong to them. Otherwise, they may throw stones at him as he goes home.

There are other spirits. The Water Dwellers live in the water and fishermen pray to them.

There are also the hunter spirits who are very handsome. Sometimes they help the hunters, but when someone trips and falls, we know one of these hunter spirits tripped him up.

Then there is Det-sata. Det-sata was once a boy who ran away from his home. He has a great many children who are all just like him and have his name. When a flock of birds flies up suddenly as if frightened, it is because Det-sata is chasing them. He is mischievous and sometimes hides an arrow from the bird hunter who may have shot it off into a perfectly clear space, but looks and looks without finding it.

Then the hunter says, "Det-sata, you have my arrow. If you do not give it up, I'll scratch you." When he looks again, he finds it.

WAR SONG

Ojibwa

From the place of the South
They come.
From the place of the South
They come.
The birds of war—
Hear the sound of their passing screams in the air.

THE WAR MEDICINE

Cherokee

Some warriors had medicine to change themselves into any animal or bird they wished.

Long ago, a warrior coming in from the hunt found enemies attacking the wigwams of his people across the river. The men were away hunting. On the river bank, he found a mussel shell. With his medicine he changed the shell into a canoe. Thus he crossed the river, and went to his grandmother's wigwam. She sat with her head in a blanket, waiting to be killed. At once he changed her into small gourd, and fastened her to his belt. Then he climbed a tree and became a swamp woodcock. Thus he flew back across the river. So the warrior and his grandmother escaped.

THE COMING OF THE WHITE MAN

Wyandot

Now in early days, the Wyandots lived about the St. Lawrence River, in the mountains to the eastward. They were the first tribe of old. They had the first chieftainship. The chief said to his nephews, the Lenapées, "Go down to the seacoast and look. If you see anything, come and tell me."

Now the Lenapées had a village by the sea. They often looked out, but they saw nothing. One day something came. When it came near the land, it stopped. Then the people were afraid. They ran into the woods. The next day two Indians went quietly to look. It was lying there in the water. Then something just like it came out of it and walked on two legs over the water.* When it came to land, two men stepped out of it. They were different from us. They made signs for the Lenapées to come out of the woods. They gave presents. Then the Lenapées gave them skin clothes.

The white men went away. They came back many times. They asked the Indians for room to put a chair on the land. So it was given. But soon they began to pull the lacing out of the bottom and to walk inland with it. They have not yet come to the end of the string.

* *A row boat.*

INDEX